Book A

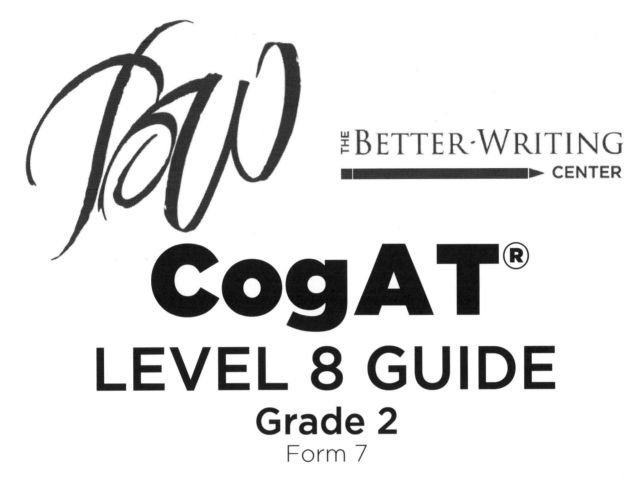

THE BETTER·WRITING CENTER

CogAT®
LEVEL 8 GUIDE
Grade 2
Form 7

By
Won Suh, J.D.
Grace Lee, M.S.

I dedicate this book to the students who purchase this book—they are the future, and it is my mission to help our younger citizens of the world step up to become great leaders one day.

How to Use This Book

This book contains 3 primary components: a study guide with examples to help you help your child understand how to approach CogAT® questions, a full-length practice test, and answers and explanations.

If this is your child's first time preparing for the CogAT®, you may want to start with the study guide and then proceed to the practice test. But if your child is familiar with the CogAT®, then you may want to consider trying the practice test first and then going over the answers and explanations; the study guide may be wholly unnecessary. I included it for the benefit of you and your child, just in case.

Study Guide's Structure

The study guide is written for you, the parent, to help your child understand the approach he or she needs to take to solve CogAT®-style questions accurately and efficiently.

The study guide is comprised of 9 sections, one for each question type. Each of the 9 sections of the study guide is comprised of 3 main parts: Structure of the Problem, Tackling the Problem, and Drills. Read these carefully and work through the drills and example problems. The answer explanations for each drill will be provided after the drill.

Practice Test's Structure

The CogAT® is comprised of 3 subtests: Verbal Battery, Quantitative Battery, and Nonverbal Battery. Each subtest is further broken down into 3 sections, for a total of 9 sections. In this book, each page of each of these 9 sections contains 2 questions. This was a deliberate design decision to better maximize the amount of visual space per problem and thereby minimize any potential confusion and room for error.

Answer Key and Explanation's Structure

The answer key and explanations are located at the back of the book. Be sure to go over the explanations to get a full understanding of how to solve the questions with your child.

Thank you and good luck!

Won Suh
Author

Contents

FREE CONSULTATION

Thank you for your purchase. Your purchase entitles you to a complimentary hour of in-person private tutoring or academic consultation.* Just bring this book!

SCHEDULE YOUR CONSULTATION TODAY
won.suh@betterwritingcenter.com

*This offer is subject to scheduling and availability limitations and will be honored on a first come, first serve basis.

TUTORING OFFERED

LEARN FROM THE BEST. LEARN FROM THE AUTHOR.

TESTING	MATHEMATICS	SCIENCE	WRITING
CogAT	Algebra 1 & 2	Biology	School Assignments
SSAT	Geometry	Chemistry	AP History DBQs
SHSAT	Trigonometry	Physics	Personal Statements
ACT	Pre-calculus	Computer Science	Application Essays
SAT	AP Calculus AB & BC		

FIND THE BETTER WRITING CENTER

THE BETTER WRITING CENTER
7369 McWhorter Place
Suite 402
Annandale, Virginia 22003

STUDY
Guide

Verbal Analogies Guide

Overview

There are 18 verbal analogies questions in the form 7, level 8 administration of the CogAT®. The student must completely fill in the bubble below the image he or she believes to be the correct answer.

Structure of the Verbal Analogies Questions

In verbal analogies questions, there are 4 squares, arranged in a 2-by-2 grid formation—that is, two squares on top and two squares on bottom. The answer choices will either be to the right or bottom of this 2-by-2 grid. The outline of a question is shown in the figure below.

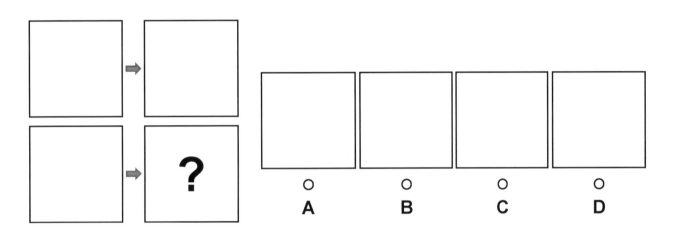

The images in the top two squares are somehow related or correlated to each other, so the images in the bottom two squares are also related to each other in a similar way.

The image in the bottom right square is not supplied and is instead replaced by a question mark. The goal of the question is to figure out which image from the answer choices replaces the question mark.

Tackling the Verbal Analogies Questions

To figure out which answer choice's image should replace the question mark, it is important to understand the relationship between the images in the top two squares of each problem. Study the top two squares in the grid.

Some common relationships are:

1. Synonyms and Antonyms
2. Use or Purpose
3. Cause and Effect
4. Characteristics and Traits in Common

What if the Answer is Not Obvious?

If there doesn't seem to be a relationship or correlation between the top two images, look instead for similarities between the images in the left squares. Then look for similarities in the image in the top right square and the images in the answer choices.

Verbal Analogies Drills

Thought Exercises

Directions: Imagine that the top left square is the first square (1), the top right square is the second (2), the bottom left square is the third (3), and the bottom right square is the fourth (4). Keeping this in mind, fill in the blanks with your own words to complete the analogy.

1. Black (1) is to white (2) as full (3) is to _____ (4).

2. Man (1) is to woman (2) as niece (3) is to _____ (4).

3. Shoe (1) is to lace (2) as balloon (3) is to _____ (4).

4. Pocket (1) is to jacket (2) as hole (3) is to _____ (4).

5. See (1) is to eye (2) as speak (3) is to _____ (4).

6. Body (1) is to soap (2) as hair (3) is to _____ (4).

7. Airplane (1) is to helicopter (2) as raft (3) is to _____ (4).

8. Cherry (1) is to tomato (2) as cucumber (3) is to _____ (4).

9. Grape (1) is to purple (2) as banana (3) is to _____ (4).

10. Meat (1) is to knife (2) as cereal (3) is to _____ (4).

11. Boot (1) is to sneaker (2) as t-shirt (3) is to _____ (4).

12. Sword (1) is to sharp (2) as grease (3) is to _____ (4).

Example CogAT® Question

Directions: Fill in the circle belonging to the image that best completes the analogy.

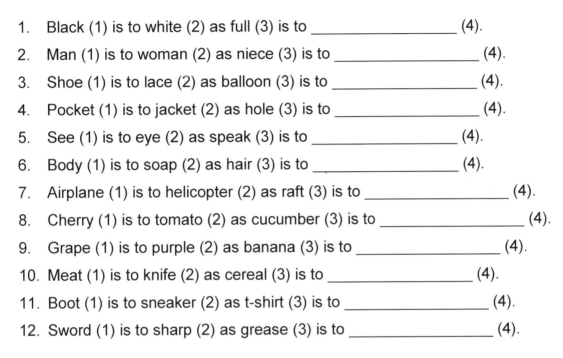

A   B   C   D

Verbal Analogies Drills Answers

Thought Exercise Answers
(Answers are samples only. Your answer, if different, may still be correct.)

1. Empty; *Explanation:* Black and white are opposite colors. Empty is the opposite of full.

2. Nephew; *Explanation:* Man and woman are gender opposites. Nephews and nieces are gender opposites.

3. String; *Explanation:* Laces tie shoes up and make sure the shoes can function properly. Balloons need to be tied up to prevent air from escaping, so that balloons can serve their intended purpose.

4. Ground; *Explanation:* A pocket is a "hole" in clothing. A hole is an indentation in the ground.

5. Mouth; *Explanation:* Seeing is done with the eyes, and speaking is done with the mouth.

6. Shampoo; *Explanation:* Soap is used to wash the body, and shampoo is used to wash hair.

7. Canoe; *Explanation:* Airplanes and helicopters are both flying vehicles. Since a raft is a vehicle that travels on water, and a canoe is another example of a vehicle that travels on water.

8. Banana; *Explanation:* Cherries and tomatoes are both round food items. Cucumbers and bananas are both elongated food items.

9. Yellow; *Explanation:* Grapes are typically purple. Bananas are typically yellow.

10. Spoon; *Explanation:* A knife is used to help us eat meat. A spoon is used to help us eat cereal.

11. Blouse; *Explanation:* Boots and sneakers are both types of footwear. T-shirts and blouses are both types of clothes worn on the upper body.

12. Slippery; *Explanation:* One of the characteristics of a sword is that it is sharp. One of the characteristics of grease is that it is slippery.

Example CogAT® Question Answer

Answer: **C**

Explanation: An axe is used to chop firewood, which is then used as fuel for fires. A handcuff is used to apprehend criminals, who are then placed in jail, behind bars. (A) would be correct if the picture in square 2 only showed firewood without the fire. (B) would be correct if square 2 showed a lumberjack. (D) is too much far removed from the analogy to be correct.

Sentence Completion Guide

Overview

There are 18 sentence completion questions in the form 7, level 8 administration of the CogAT®. The student must completely fill in the bubble below the image he or she believes to be the correct answer.

Structure of the Sentence Completion Questions

In sentence completion questions, a question is asked in quotations, followed by the answer choices.

The questions are parsed in the form of, "Which one is ...?" so that it is possible to answer each question by picking the correct image.

Tackling the Sentence Completion Questions

The first thing to do when solving a sentence completion question is to identify the key word or words of the question. That is, there should be one or two pivotal words that define

Further, because the question can be wholly answered by choosing a single image, each question is generally limited in what it can ask about.

Broadly speaking, the scope of the questions are limited to:

1. Purpose and Function
2. Categorization and Description
3. Characteristics and Traits

A purpose and function question may look like, "Which one is used for..." or "Which one can do..."

A categorization and description question may look like, "Which one belongs to..."

A characteristics and traits question may look like, "Which one looks..." or "Which one is similar to..."

In one sense, the sentence completion questions are the easiest, but in another sense they are not. They are the easiest in that they are the most direct. They are potentially the most difficult if the words that appear in the question are unfamiliar to the student; the student is at the mercy of the test writers.

Having your child read many books is one of the best ways to assure that your child's repertoire of vocabulary words remains robust.

What if the Answer is Not Obvious?

If it seems more than one image can be the answer to the question, it is important to look for the differences between the images. Sometimes, even small differences can be the difference between the correct answer and an incorrect one.

If your child does not know the key word(s) at all, then instead of instructing him or her to guess blindly, instruct him or her to see if he or she can find the image that is most dissimilar to the other images. Sometimes, even if the correct answer is not obvious, the most different answer can be the correct answer. That is, if the other choices all share some common similarity, but one doesn't, the odd choice out can be the correct answer. Of course, this is not a foolproof approach, but it certainly is one strategy to consider.

Sentence Completion Drills

Thought Exercises
Directions: Answer the following questions by circling the letter in front of the best answer choice.

1. "Which one is found in outer space?"
   A. Sky   B. Lake   C. Moon   D. Plants

2. "Which one has the longest neck?"
   A. Human   B. Giraffe   C. Elephant   D. Lizard

3. "Which one is not a holiday?"
   A. Christmas   B. Easter   C. Birthday   D. Thanksgiving

4. "Which one helps to see farther?"
   A. Telescope   B. Television   C. Telegraph   D. Telephone

5. "Which one neighs?"
   A. Fish   B. Horse   C. Person   D. Blue Jay

6. "Which one is worn around the neck?"
   A. Belt   B. Cap   C. Ring   D. Scarf

7. "Which one is the fastest on land?"
   A. Worm   B. Rabbit   C. Snail   D. Turtle

8. "Which one is used in archery?"
   A. Bow   B. Club   C. Puck   D. Cleat

Example CogAT® Question
Directions: Fill in the circle under the image that best answers the question.

"Which one does a veterinarian help?"

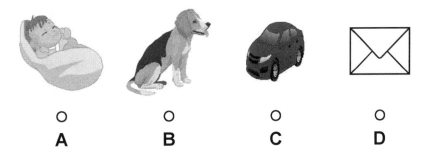

   O   O   O   O
   A   **B**   **C**   **D**

Sentence Completion Drills Answers

Thought Exercise Answers

1. C, Moon; *Explanation:* The sky, lakes, and plants are all contained within the Earth and its atmosphere.

2. B, Giraffe; *Explanation:* Giraffes have longer necks than humans, elephants, and lizards. Elephants have long trunks, but those are not necks.

3. C, Birthday; *Explanation:* Christmas, Easter, and Thanksgiving are all established holidays. The word "Birthday" is too general to indicate a holiday, even though many holidays do in fact celebrate famous people's birthdays.

4. A, Telescope; *Explanation:* Telescopes help people see farther than they could with their naked eye. Television is something we watch. Telephones are speaking devices. Telegraphs were machines used to send messages.

5. B, Horse; *Explanation:* Neighing is a type of sound a horse makes. None of the other animals neigh.

6. D, Scarf; *Explanation:* A scarf is an article of clothing worn around the neck to protect it from the cold or other elements. Belts are worn around the waist; caps are worn on the head; and rings are worn on the fingers.

7. B, Rabbit; *Explanation:* Snails, turtles, and worms are not faster than rabbits on land. Also, snails, turtles, and worms have reputations for being slow-moving.

8. A, Bow; *Explanation:* Archery is a sport that mainly uses a bow and arrows. A club is used in golf, a puck is used in hockey, and a cleat is a type of shoe used in various sports involving moving on grass, turf, or dirt surfaces, but it is not used in archery. Soccer, American football, lacrosse, and baseball are commonly played sports that make use of cleats.

Example CogAT® Question Answer

Answer: **B**

Explanation: A veterinarian is a doctor who takes care of animals. Since answer choice B is the only one that shows an animal, B is the correct answer. Veterinarians do not take care of human babies.

Verbal Classification Guide

Overview

There are 18 verbal classification questions in the form 7, level 8 administration of the CogAT®. The student must completely fill in the bubble below the image he or she believes to be the correct answer.

Structure of the Verbal Classification Questions

In verbal classification questions, there are 2 rows of images. The top row images make up the question. The bottom row is comprised of the answer choices and their images. The 2 rows are separated by line to reduce confusion. The outline of a question is shown in the figure below. Imagine that each square contains an image. Note that the actual questions will not necessarily contain the squares shown below.

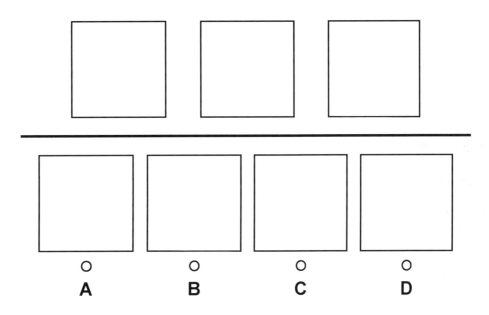

Tackling the Verbal Analogy Questions

The images in the top row are somehow alike in one way or another. The goal is to figure out which image among the answer choices belongs in the top row. Study the three images in the top row to find similarities between them.

Some similarities to take note of are:

1. Shape, Size, and Color
2. Use, Function, or Purpose
3. Object Classification
4. Characteristics and Traits

19

Find as many similarities as possible between the images of the top row. If there are, for instance, 2 similarities that all of the images in the top row share, then there is a great likelihood that the correct answer will share the same 2 similarities. The more specific the similarity, the better.

What if the Answer is Not Obvious?

If it seems more than one image can be the answer to the question, try counting the number of similarities there are between each of the answer choices and the images in the top row. The image with the most number of similarities will probably be the correct answer.

Verbal Classification Drills

Thought Exercises

Directions: Answer each of the following questions by circling the word that **least** belongs in the group of words.

1.	Printer	Monitor	Keyboard	Lamp	Speaker
2.	Mouse	Rat	Fox	Squirrel	Chipmunk
3.	Soldier	Politician	Teacher	Hero	Doctor
4.	Box	Ball	Wheel	Bowl	Globe
5.	Lemon	Lime	Peach	Grapefruit	Orange
6.	Cupcake	Brownie	Candy	Pie	Cola
7.	Pencil	Cabinet	Notepad	Stapler	Marker
8.	Shorts	Parka	Shoes	Socks	Jeans
9.	Lake	Mountain	Tower	Valley	River
10.	Bottle	Jar	Bin	Lid	Box

Example CogAT® Question

Directions: Answer the following question by filling in the bubble below the image that most belongs with the images in the top row.

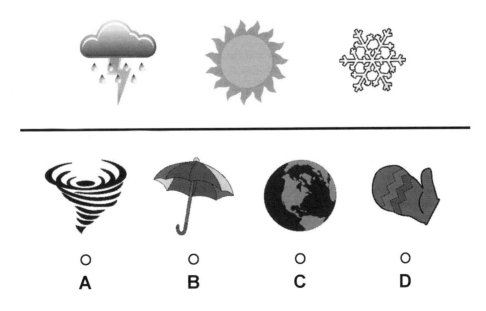

A   B   C   D

21

Verbal Classification Drills Answers

Thought Exercise Answers

1. Lamp; *Explanation:* A printer, monitor, keyboard, and speaker are all computer peripherals. A lamp is not considered a computer peripheral. That is, a lamp does not enhance or permit the functionality of a computer.

2. Fox; *Explanation:* Fox is the only animal listed that is not a rodent. Mouse, Rat, Squirrel, and Chipmunk are all examples of rodents.

3. Hero; *Explanation:* Being a hero is not by itself a career. The other examples (soldier, politician, teacher, and doctor) are all of careers.

4. Box; *Explanation:* The other objects listed have some roundness to them. Boxes are not rounded. Thus, a box has the least in common with the other answer choices.

5. Peach; *Explanation:* Peaches are not citrus fruits, while lemons, limes, grapefruits, and oranges are.

6. Cola; *Explanation:* Cola is the only beverage snack item. It is not a solid food like the other options are.

7. Cabinet; *Explanation:* Cabinets are not office supplies like the other items are. Cabinets are furniture pieces.

8. Parka; *Explanation:* A parka is a type of coat with a hood, so it is worn on the upper body. The other clothes items listed are worn on the lower body.

9. Tower; *Explanation:* A tower is a manmade construct. The other things are found naturally in the environment or landscape.

10. Lid; *Explanation:* A lid closes a container, but it is not meant to hold or store things like the other items listed are meant to.

Example CogAT® Question Answer

Answer: **A**

Explanation: The items in the question relate to or describe natural weather conditions. A tornado is also a natural weather condition. An umbrella is used when it is raining, but it is not a weather condition. A globe or Earth does not describe or relate to a weather condition. A glove or mitten is an article of clothing worn when it is cold, but neither is a weather condition.

Number Analogies Guide

Overview

There are 18 number analogies questions in the form 7, level 8 administration of the CogAT®. The student must completely fill in the bubble below the image he or she believes to be the correct answer.

Structure of the Number Analogies Questions

In number analogies questions, there are 4 squares, arranged in a 2-by-2 grid formation—that is, two squares on top and two squares on bottom. The answer choices will either be to the right or bottom of this 2-by-2 grid. The outline of a question is shown in the figure below.

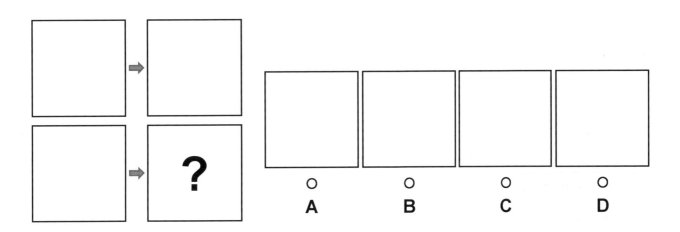

The numbers of objects or images in the top two squares are numerically related or correlated, so the numbers of objects or images in the bottom two squares are also related to each other in a similar way.

The bottom right square contains a question mark. The goal of the question is to figure out which answer choice replaces the question mark.

Tackling the Number Analogies Questions

To figure out which answer choice should replace the question mark, it is important to understand the number relationship between the images in the top two squares of each problem.

Study the top two squares in the grid and count the number of objects in the first square. Then count the number of objects in the second square and see how they might be related. The types of objects or images can be different. It's important to focus mostly on the numbers.

Ask the following question: How much needs to be added or subtracted from the top left square to get the number of objects or images found in the top right square?

Compare the answer choices to the bottom left square. If none of the answer choices seems to work, then think about either multiplying or dividing, as needed.

What if the Answer is Not Obvious?

If the answer is still not apparent, it is possible that a combination of multiplication or division and addition or subtraction is needed.

Furthermore, it may be possible that the correct answer does not follow the same pattern, but the inverse pattern, as long as the difference in the number of objects in the answer and the number of objects in the bottom left square is the same as the difference in the numbers of objects in the top two squares. *Only use this approach when positive that all other approaches are incorrect.*

Number Analogies Drills

Thought Exercises

Directions: For each question, circle the answer choice that best completes the number analogy.

1. One is to Three as Five is to _____.
   A. Two   B. Four   C. Six   D. Seven

2. Four is to Seven as Two is to _____.
   A. Eight   B. Seven   C. Five   D. Four

3. Five is to One as Seven is to _____.
   A. Six   B. Three   C. Two   D. One

4. Six is to Three as Eight is to _____.
   A. Five   B. Six   C. Seven   D. Nine

5. Two is to Four as Three is to _____.
   A. One   B. Two   C. Four   D. Six

6. One is to Three as Three is to _____.
   A. Three   B. Six   C. Nine   D. Ten

7. Seven is to Eight as Six is to _____.
   A. Nine   B. Five   C. Four   D. Two

8. Four is to Nine as Three is to _____.
   A. Four   B. Five   C. Six   D. Seven

Example CogAT® Question

Directions: Fill in the circle below the answer choice of the image that best completes the analogy.

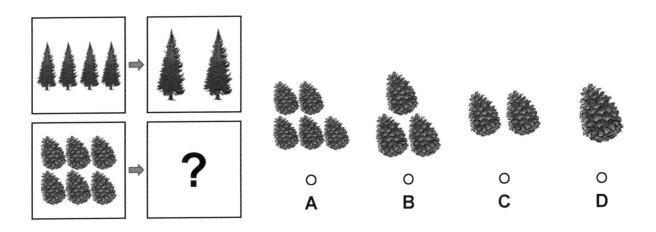

Number Analogies Drills Answers

Thought Exercise Answers

1. D, Seven; *Explanation:* 1 + **2** = 3, and 5 + **2** = 7.

2. C, Five; *Explanation:* 4 + **3** = 7, and 2 + **3** = 5.

3. B, Three; *Explanation:* 5 − **4** = 1, and 7 − **4** = 3.

4. A, Five; *Explanation:* 6 − **3** = 3, and 8 − **3** = 5.

5. D, Six; *Explanation:* 2 × **2** = 4, and 3 × **2** = 6. Note that the other choices don't work. 2 + 2 = 4, but there is no answer choice of 5, so it can't be 3 + 2 = 5. Thus, we can eliminate + 2 as the operation that needs to be performed.

6. C, Nine; *Explanation:* 1 × **3** = 3, and 3 × **3** = 9. Note that the other choices don't work. 1 + 2 = 3, but there is no answer choice of 5, so it can't be 3 + 2 = 5. Thus, we can eliminate + 2 as the operation that needs to be performed.

7. B, Five; *Explanation:* 7 + **1** = 8, and 6 − **1** = 5. Ordinarily, the answer should appear as 7. However, 7 isn't one of the answer choices. Then we must realize that the relationship is that there is a difference of 1 between the numbers. Thus, 5 is the best fit to complete the analogy.

8. D, Seven; *Explanation:* 4 × **2** + **1** = 9, and 3 × **2** + **1** = 7. Ordinarily, the answer should be 8, as 4 + 5 = 9, and 3 + 5 = 8. Eight is not an answer choice, however, so it is important to switch to another way of thinking about the relationship between 4 and 9.

Example CogAT® Question Answer

Answer: **B**

Explanation: 4 ÷ 2 = 2, and 6 ÷ 2 = 3. 4 − 2 = 2 is also a valid way to think about this analogy, but 6 − 2 = 4, and 4 pine cones isn't an answer choice. That's how we know the relationship between the trees isn't one of addition or subtraction.

Number Puzzles Guide

Overview

There are 14 number puzzles questions in the form 7, level 8 administration of the CogAT®. The student must completely fill in the bubble below the image he or she believes to be the correct answer.

Structure of the Number Puzzles Questions

In number puzzles questions, there are 2 trains separated by a vertical line. Each side of this line represents a side of a mathematical equation. Thus, both sides combined make up a full equation.

One of the trains (very likely to be the one on the left side of the vertical line) is depicted as carrying a certain number of cargo items. The other train on the other side of the vertical line has more cars (usually 2 in total) and a fewer number of cargo items—one of this train's cars contains the cargo items and the other contains a question mark. The outline of a number puzzle question is shown below.

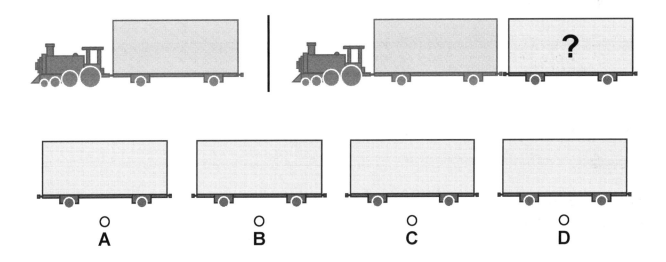

The goal is to determine which answer choice should replace the car containing the question mark by figuring out how many cargo items the mystery car should contain.

Tackling the Number Puzzles Questions

Think of number puzzles questions as addition or subtraction problems. To find the correct answer, determine how many more cargo objects must be added to the right train in order to make it carry the same number of cargo objects as the left train is carrying.

Count the number of items the left train is carrying and subtract that by the number of objects the right train is already carrying. This will give you the answer to how many objects the left train's mystery car should carry.

If the answer is not obvious at first, then try recounting the number of objects and making sure the subtraction or addition was done correctly.

Number Puzzles Drills

Thought Exercises

Directions: For each question, write in the correct answer to satisfy the equation.

1. $7 = 4 +$ _____

2. $3 = 1 +$ _____

3. $6 = 3 +$ _____

4. $9 = 0 +$ _____

5. $4 +$ _____ $= 9$

6. $5 +$ _____ $= 11$

7. $1 +$ _____ $= 10$

8. $6 +$ _____ $= 19$

9. _____ $+ 4 = 12$

10. _____ $+ 6 = 6$

11. _____ $+ 7 = 14$

12. _____ $+ 11 = 22$

13. $12 = 3 + 7 +$ _____

14. $17 = 5 + 6 +$ _____

15. $2 +$ _____ $+ 5 = 8$

16. $7 +$ _____ $+ 9 = 20$

17. _____ $+ 3 + 1 = 13$

18. _____ $+ 8 + 8 = 18$

Example CogAT® Question

Directions: Choose the answer choice that is needed to give the second train the same number of objects as the first train.

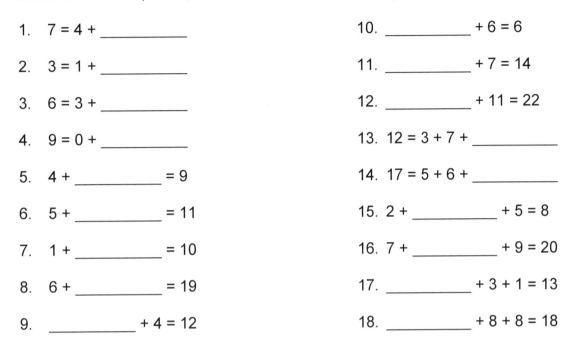

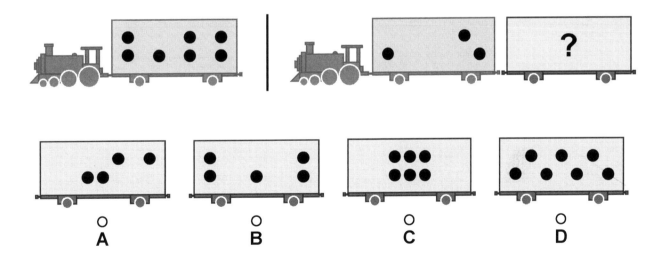

A   B   C   D

29

Number Puzzles Drills Answers

Thought Exercise Answers

1. 3; *Explanation:* 7 = 4 + 3.

2. 2; *Explanation:* 3 = 1 + 2.

3. 3; *Explanation:* 6 = 3 + 3.

4. 9; *Explanation:* 9 = 0 + 9.

5. 5; *Explanation:* 4 + 5 = 9.

6. 6; *Explanation:* 5 + 6 = 11.

7. 9; *Explanation:* 1 + 9 = 10.

8. 13; *Explanation:* 6 + 13 = 19.

9. 8; *Explanation:* 8 + 4 = 12.

10. 0; *Explanation:* 0 + 6 = 6.

11. 7; *Explanation:* 7 + 7 = 14.

12. 11; *Explanation:* 11 + 11 = 22.

13. 2; *Explanation:* 12 = 3 + 7 + 2.

14. 6; *Explanation:* 17 = 5 + 6 + 6.

15. 1; *Explanation:* 2 + 1 + 5 = 8.

16. 4; *Explanation:* 7 + 4 + 9 = 20.

17. 9; *Explanation:* 9 + 3 + 1 = 13.

18. 2; *Explanation:* 2 + 8 + 8 = 18.

Example CogAT® Question Answer

Answer: **A**

Explanation: The left train is carrying 7 objects. The first car of the right train is carrying 3. This means that the second car of the right train must be carrying 4 objects, since 7 = 3 + 4 or 7 − 3 = 4.

Number Series Guide

Overview

There are 18 number series questions in the form 7, level 8 administration of the CogAT®. The student must completely fill in the bubble below the image he or she believes to be the correct answer.

Structure of the Number Series Questions

In number series questions, there is an abacus that contains columns of beads or circles. A sample question template is shown below. (On the actual test, the answer choices may be to the right of the abacus.)

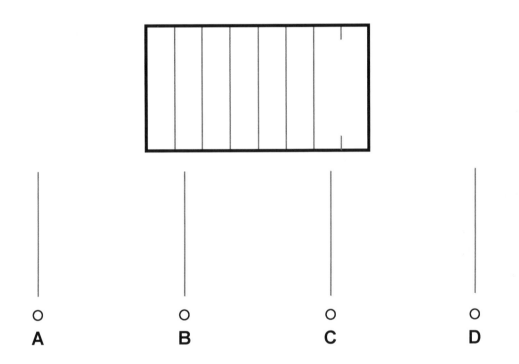

The last column of beads is missing beads, so the goal is to find the correct number of beads that should occupy that column.

Tackling the Number Series Questions

Number series questions can be answered by finding the pattern of the number of beads. Count the number of beads in the columns. Then compare the numbers of beads in the columns.

Look for some of the following common patterns for the numbers of beads:

1. Straight pattern: the number of beads increases or decreases by a set amount with each column move to the right.
2. Leapfrog pattern: the number of beads increases or decreases by a set amount every other column, while the other columns retain the same number.
3. Alternating patterns: two patterns exist concurrently in an alternating fashion, such that the odd numbered columns adhere to one pattern while the even numbered columns adhere to another.

What if the Answer is Not Obvious?

If the answer is still not apparent, try to think outside the box. Look for other patterns that do not necessarily conform to the common patterns listed above. Work through the thought exercises on the next page to get a better feel for the more "unorthodox" problems.

Number Series Drills

Thought Exercises

Directions: Given the numbers, find the next number in the pattern.

1. 4, 5, 6, 7, 8, 9, _____.

2. 2, 4, 6, 8, 10, 12, _____.

3. 0, 3, 6, 9, 12, 15, _____.

4. 2, 3, 5, 3, 8, 3, _____.

5. 3, 4, 6, 9, 13, 18, _____.

6. 1, 1, 2, 3, 5, 8, _____.

7. 2, 1, 4, 3, 6, 5, _____.

8. 15, 13, 11, 9, 7, 5, _____.

9. 4, 4, 5, 5, 6, 6, _____.

10. 7, 6, 5, 7, 6, 5, _____.

Example CogAT® Question

Directions: Fill in the circle below the column of beads that would appear next in the series.

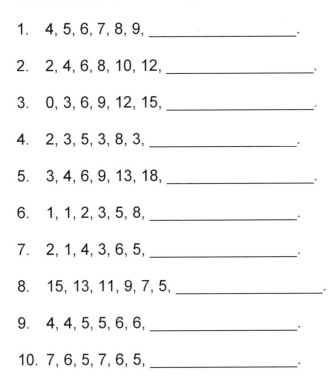

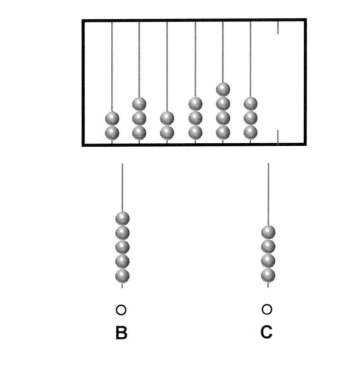

Number Series Drills Answers

Thought Exercise Answers

1. 10; *Explanation:* The numbers increase by 1. 9 + 1 = 10.

2. 14; *Explanation:* The numbers increase by 2. 12 + 2 = 14.

3. 18; *Explanation:* The numbers increase by 3. 15 + 3 = 18.

4. 11; *Explanation:* The odd numbered terms increase by 3, while the even numbered terms stay constant at 3. The 7th term is 8 + 3 = 11.

5. 24; *Explanation:* The differences between the terms increases by 1 each time. The difference between 3 and 4 is 1. The difference between 4 and 6 is 2. The difference 6 and 9 is 3. The difference between 9 and 13 is 4. The difference between 13 and 18 is 5. The difference between 18 and the next term should be 6, then. 18 + 6 = 24.

6. 13; *Explanation:* Starting with the third term, the value of the term is the sum of the previous two terms. 1 + 1 = 2; 1 + 2 = 3; 2 + 3 = 5; 3 + 5 = 8; 5 + 8 = 13.

7. 8; *Explanation:* The terms are increasing by 2, but the odd terms start at 2, and the even terms start at 1. Since we're looking for the 7th term, we focus on the 5th term and add 2 to the term: 6 + 2 = 8.

8. 3; *Explanation:* The numbers are decreasing by 2. 5 – 2 = 3.

9. 7; *Explanation:* Each number is repeated twice, starting at 4. The next number after 6, which is repeated twice, is 7.

10. 7; *Explanation:* The numbers 7, 6, and 5 repeat in a cycle. Since the 6th number ended with a 5, the cycle of 7, 6, and 5 will start again. The next number after 5 is 7.

Example CogAT® Question Answer

Answer: **C**

Explanation: The numbers of beads in the abacus can be expressed as 2, 3, 2, 3, 4, 3. Notice the numbers can be broken up into 2, 3, 2 and 3, 4, 3. Each of the numbers in the second set is one bigger than each of the corresponding numbers in the first set of three numbers. The next set of numbers would likely be 4, 5, 4, so 4 would be the 7th number and therefore the correct answer.

Figure Matrices Guide

Overview

There are 18 figure matrices questions in the form 7, level 8 administration of the CogAT®. The student must completely fill in the bubble below the image he or she believes to be the correct answer.

Structure of the Figure Matrices Questions

In figure matrices questions, there are 4 squares, arranged in a 2-by-2 grid formation—that is, two squares on top and two squares on bottom. The answer choices will either be to the right or bottom of this 2-by-2 grid. The outline of a question is shown in the figure below.

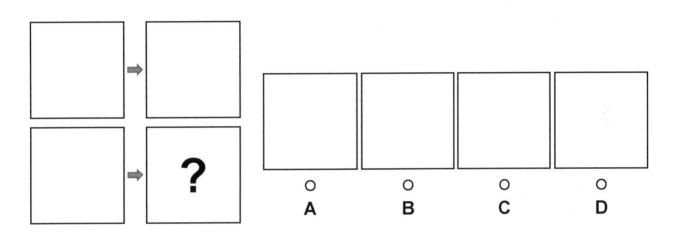

The figures or shapes in the top two squares are related or correlated in some way, so the numbers of objects or images in the bottom two squares are also related to each other in a similar way.

The bottom right square contains a question mark. The goal of the question is to figure out which answer choice replaces the question mark.

Tackling the Figure Matrices Questions

In solving figure matrices questions, look for the relationships and similarities between the shapes or figures in the top squares of the question. Some of the relationships and similarities to look for are:

1. Shape and Number of Sides
2. Arrangement of Figures
3. Color and Shading
4. Size
5. Rotations

Figure Matrices Drills

Thought Exercises

Directions: For each question, a figure is provided to the right of the question. Redraw the figure according to all three of the conditions stated.

1. A. Size of Side Lengths: 0.5x (Half)
   B. Color and Shading: None
   C. Rotation: None

2. A. Size of Side Lengths: 2x (Double)
   B. Color and Shading: Gray
   C. Rotation: None

3. A. Size of Side Lengths: 1x (Same)
   B. Color and Shading: Light Gray
   C. Rotation: 180°

4. A. Size of Side Lengths: 0.5x (Half)
   B. Color and Shading: None
   C. Rotation: 90° Clockwise

5. A. Size of Side Lengths: 2x (Double)
   B. Color and Shading: Black
   C. Rotation: 45° Counterclockwise

Example CogAT® Question

Directions: Choose the answer choice that best completes the analogy.

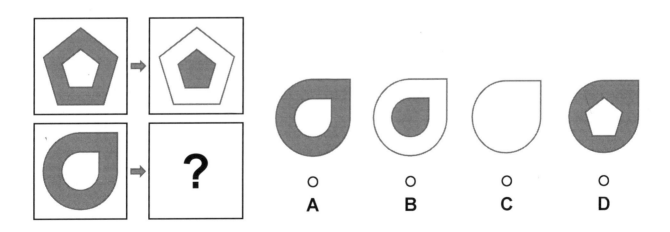

Number Puzzles Drills Answers

Thought Exercise Answers

1.

Explanation: The side lengths of the square above are half the size of the original's on the previous page. The square has not been colored or rotated.

2.

Explanation: The side lengths of the pentagon above are double the size of the original's on the previous page. The pentagon has also been shaded gray. It has not been rotated.

3.

Explanation: The side lengths of triangle above are the same size as the original's on the previous page. The triangle has been shaded in a light gray. The triangle has also been rotated 180° (or a full upside-down flip).

4.

Explanation: The dimensions of the oval and square above are half the size of the original's on the previous page. The figure has not been shaded. It has been rotated 90° clockwise.

5.

Explanation: The side lengths of the square above are double the size of the original's on the previous page. The square has also been shaded gray. It has been rotated 45°. (For this exercise, it doesn't matter whether the figure was rotated clockwise or counterclockwise.)

Example CogAT® Question Answer

Answer: **B**

Explanation: The top left square in the question shows a dark pentagon with a smaller white pentagon nested inside. The top right square shows the same figure, except with the shading inverted. The bottom left square shows a dark teardrop-like shape with a smaller white one nested inside. The correct answer is thus the figure that shows the same figure but with its colors inverted.

Paper Folding Guide

Overview

There are 14 paper folding questions in the form 7, level 8 administration of the CogAT®. The student must completely fill in the bubble below the image he or she believes to be the correct answer.

Structure of the Paper Folding Questions

Paper folding questions start with a diagram of a square sheet of paper. This square is folded once or more, either horizontally, vertically, or diagonally. After the paper is finished being folded, one or more holes are punched into the paper. The purpose of paper folding questions is to figure out how many holes the square sheet of paper will have when it is fully unfolded.

Below are the ways that a paper can be single-folded:

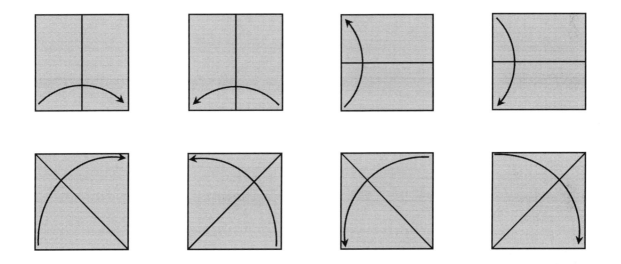

After the first fold, you may see a second fold on the test. Below are some of the ways a second fold can happen:

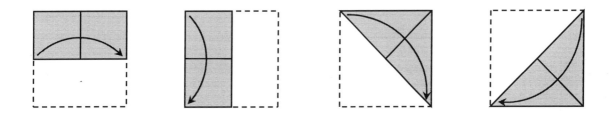

Tackling the Paper Folding Questions

In solving paper folding questions, it is important to be able to understand and identify the lines of symmetry for the folding. Luckily, the fold lines are the lines of symmetry.

The first key to solving paper folding questions is realizing that each time the paper is unfolded, the number of holes in the paper is double the number of holes that were in the paper before the paper is unfolded.

The second key to solving paper folding questions is realizing that the second set of holes is a mirror reflection of the first set of holes but across the fold line. This means that the two sets of holes are directly opposite from each other across the fold line. Furthermore, the corresponding holes are equidistant from the fold line.

Tip: Starting from the center of each hole, draw a line perpendicular* to the fold line. For each perpendicular line you drew, draw a line of equal length and opposite direction from the fold line. You will now have the locations of all of the circles' centers. Draw the circles around their centers, and you will have the image of the paper as it should look after the holes are punched.

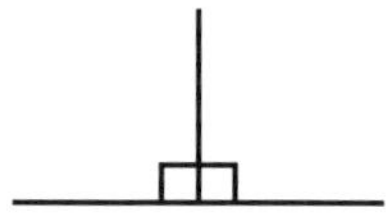

*Note: Two perpendicular lines intersect, or meet, to create 90° angles (as shown in the diagram on the right). Of course, 2nd and 3rd grade students may not be familiar with the concept of perpendicular lines and 90° angles. It may be easier to explain to children to draw a line until they make a 'T' with the fold line and then to draw another congruent line from the fold line to make another 'T' that is on the opposite side of the fold line.

Paper Folding Drills

Thought Exercises
Directions: For each question, draw the mirror image of the shape or figure across fold line.

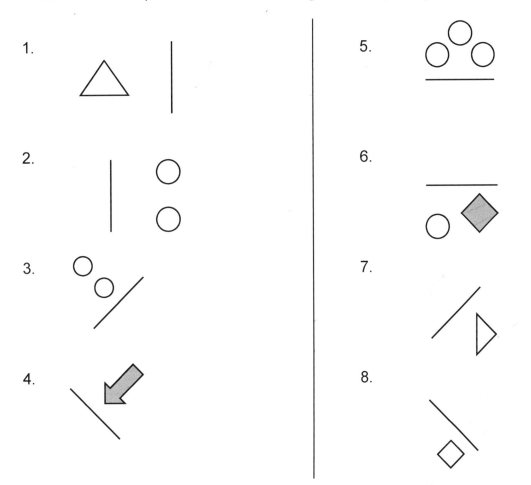

1.

2.

3.

4.

5.

6.

7.

8.

Example CogAT® Question
Directions: Fill in the circle below the image of the paper as it would look unfolded all the way.

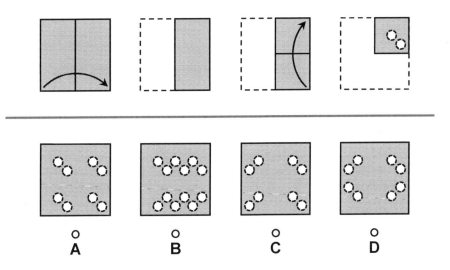

O
A

O
B

O
C

O
D

Paper Folding Drills Answers

Thought Exercise Answers

Explanation: Draw a perpendicular line from each vertex (or center, if it's a circle) of the figure to the fold line. Then, for each line drawn to the fold line, draw a congruent perpendicular line from the fold line to the other side of the fold line. Then connect the vertices, or draw a circle, to create the mirror image (shown here in dotted lines).

1.

5.

2.

6.

3.

7.

8.

4.

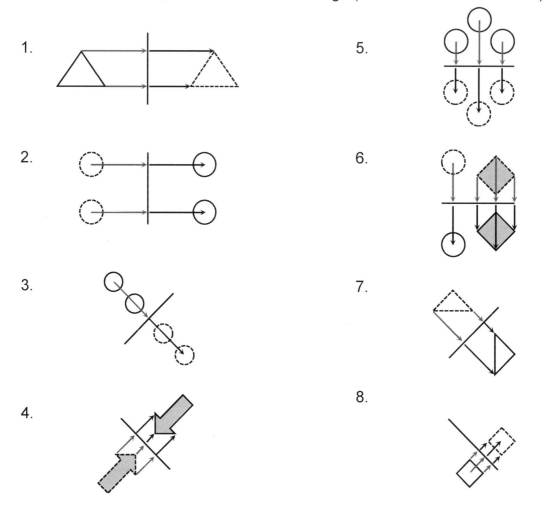

Example CogAT® Question Answer

Answer: **D**

Explanation: Using the perpendicular line method described in guide, we see that after unfolding the paper once, there should be 4 holes:

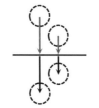

Use the perpendicular line method again, but this time for all 4 holes. This will lead to 4 more holes, for a total of 8 holes, in the configuration of the correct answer.

Figure Classification Guide

Overview

There are 18 figure classification questions in the form 7, level 8 administration of the CogAT®. The student must completely fill in the bubble below the image he or she believes to be the correct answer.

Structure of the Figure Classification Questions

In figure classification questions, there are 2 sets of images. The sets are separated by a dividing line to reduce confusion. The images in the first set comprise the question and the images in the second set comprise the answer choices.

In this book, each question has been arranged into 2 rows, with the top set comprising the question and the bottom set comprising the answer choices. An outline of a question has been provided below to show the structure of how the questions are formatted in this book.

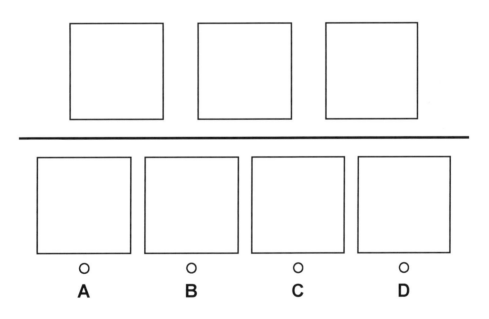

On the actual test itself, the question set and the answer choice set may be all arranged on the same row, with the question set to the left of the dividing line and the answer choice set to the line's right.

Regardless of the layout of the questions, the logic behind the questions is all the same. The images in the question set are all related in some way. That is, they are all similar in at least one way.

Tackling the Figure Classification Questions

In solving figure classification questions, take note of:

1. Shape
2. Size
3. Color or Shading
4. Patterns

Find as many similarities as possible between the images of the question set. If there are, for instance, 2 similarities that all of the images in the top row share, then there is a great likelihood that the correct answer will share the same 2 similarities. The more specific the similarity or similarities, the better.

What if the Answer is Not Obvious?

If it seems more than one image can be the answer to the question, try counting the number of similarities there are between each of the answer choices and the images in the top row. The image with the most number of similarities will probably be the correct answer.

Figure Classification Drills

Thought Exercises

Directions: For each question, draw a circle around the figure that **least** belongs in the group.

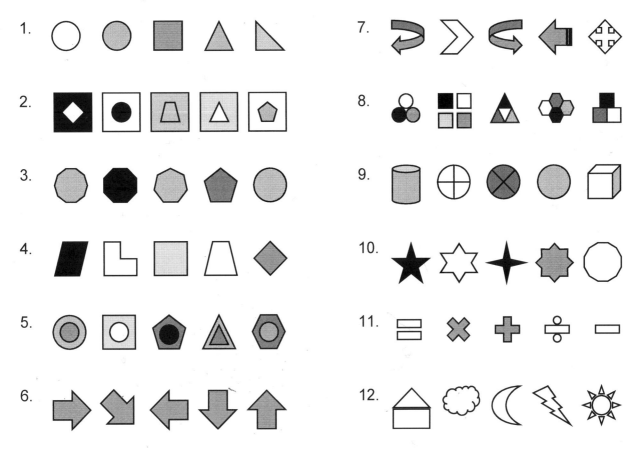

Example CogAT® Question

Directions: Fill in the circle below the image of figure that belongs in the top row.

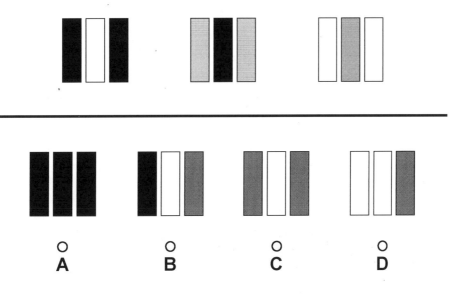

Figure Classification Drills Answers

Thought Exercise Answers

1.

   Explanation: This is the only unshaded figure.

2.

   Explanation: This is the only figure whose interior figure's color is the same as the exterior figure's color.

3.

   Explanation: This is the only figure that isn't a polygon; that is, it is only figure that doesn't have edges.

4.

   Explanation: This is the only figure that is not a quadrilateral.

5.

   Explanation: This is the only figure whose interior figure is not a circle.

6.

   Explanation: This is the only figure that is not pointing in a cardinal direction (up, down, left, right).

7.

   Explanation: This is the only figure that is pointing in more than one direction.

8.

   Explanation: This is the only figure whose smaller figures aren't touching.

9.

   Explanation: This is the only figure that doesn't have any circles in its shape.

10.

    Explanation: This is the only figure that is perfectly convex, meaning that there aren't any "indentations" or dips in the sides or edges.

11.

    Explanation: This is the only figure that isn't an arithmetic operator. It is also the only one whose figures are unconnected.

12.

    Explanation: This is the only figure that does not have anything to do with nature or weather.

Example CogAT® Question Answer

Answer: **C**

Explanation: In each of figures in the top row, the leftmost and rightmost bars are the same color, and the middle bar is a different color. The figure in (C) is the only one that follows this pattern.

PRACTICE
Test

VERBAL
Battery

VERBAL
ANALOGIES

DIRECTIONS & EXAMPLE QUESTION

The following directions are to be used for all verbal analogies questions:

Directions: For each question, in the grid of 4 squares, the top two figures are related in some way. Choose the answer choice that goes with the bottom left figure in a similar way.

Below is an example verbal analogies question:

Explanation: A plane is a vehicle that flies and eagle is an animal that flies. A sailboat is a vehicle that travels in water. None of the answer choices fits perfectly, as none of the animals are completely aquatic. But of the answer choices, A works the best because beavers by nature spend a significant time in and around water.

Question 1

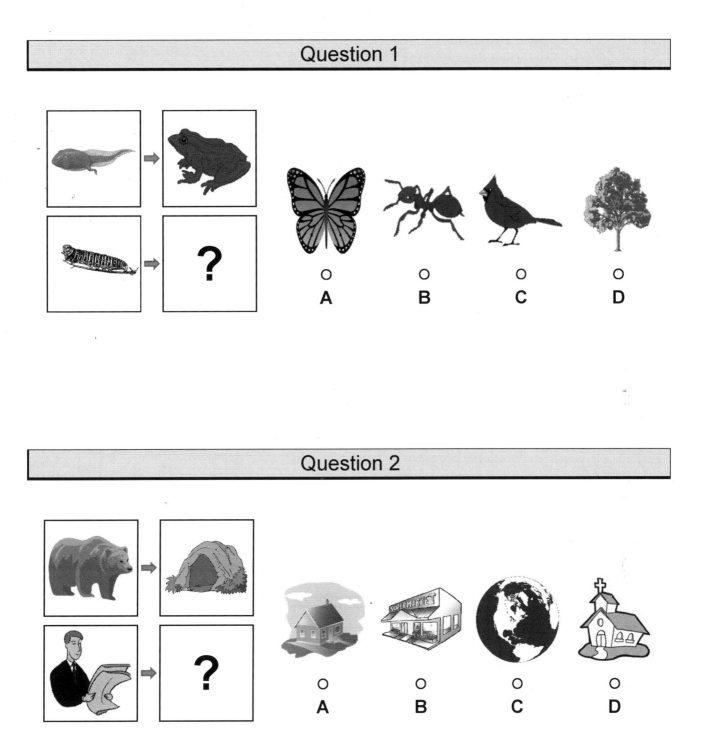

Question 2

Question 3

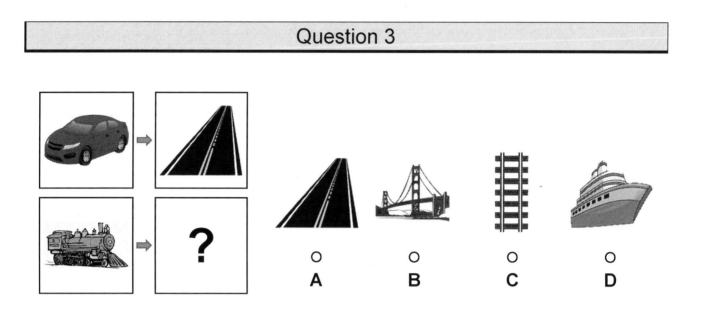

O	O	O	O
A	B	C	D

Question 4

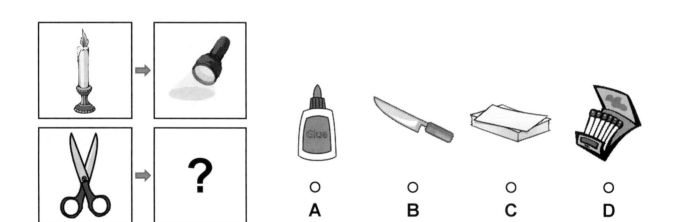

O	O	O	O
A	B	C	D

Question 5

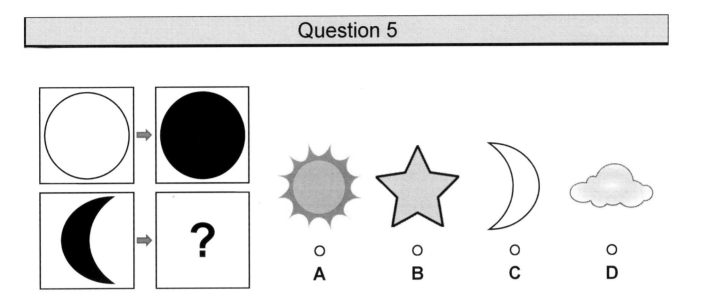

Question 6

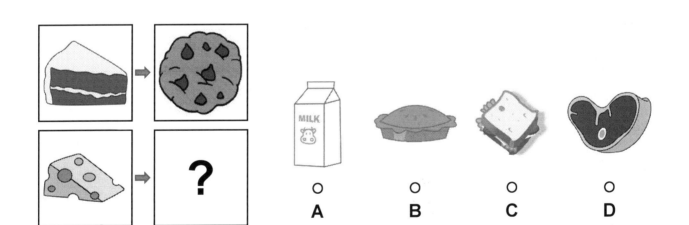

Question 7

A   B   C   D

Question 8

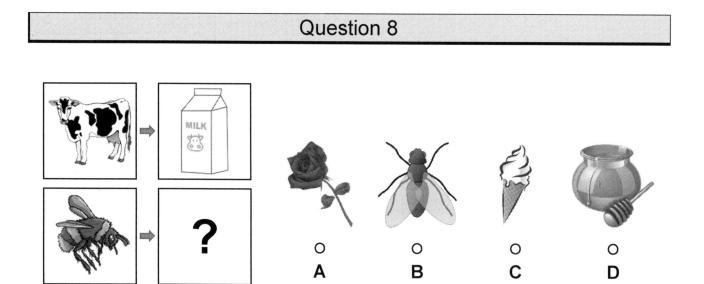

A   B   C   D

Question 9

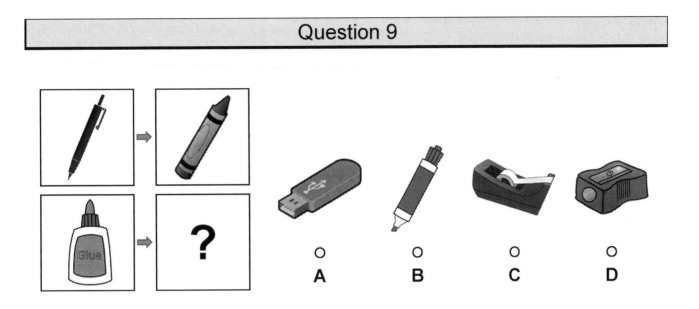

Question 10

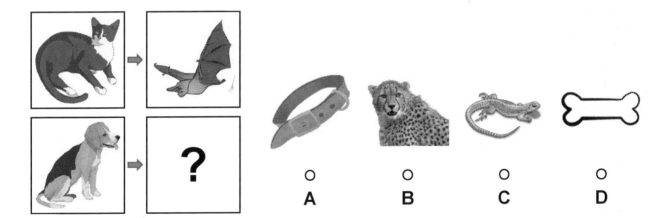

Question 11

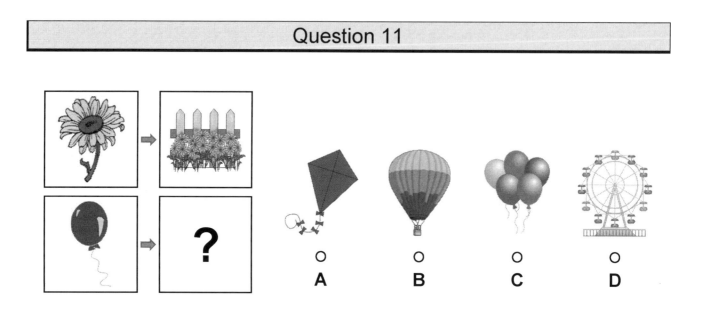

A   B   C   D

Question 12

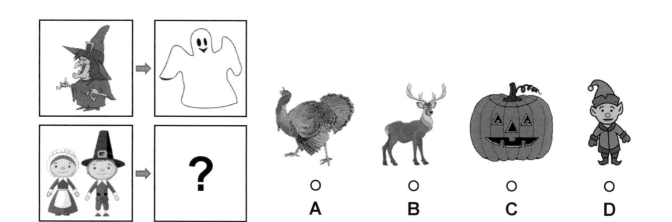

A   B   C   D

Question 13

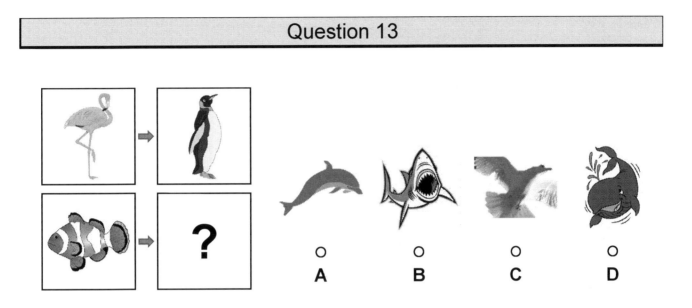

Question 14

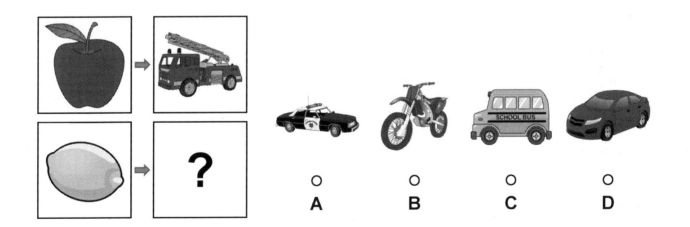

Question 15

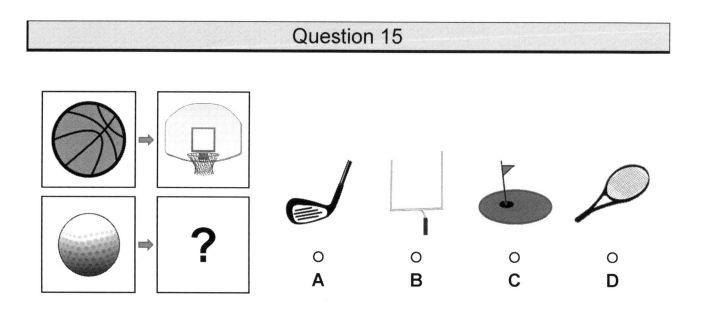

A B C D

Question 16

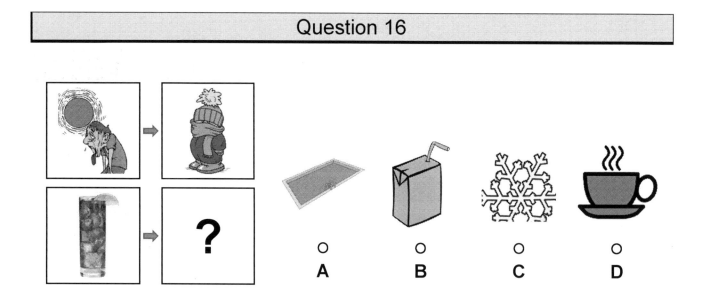

A B C D

Question 17

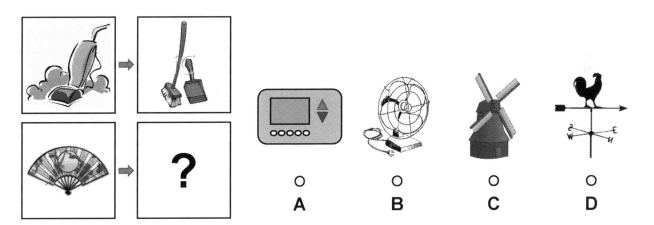

○　　　　　○　　　　　○　　　　　○
A　　　　　B　　　　　C　　　　　D

Question 18

○　　　　　○　　　　　○　　　　　○
A　　　　　B　　　　　C　　　　　D

SENTENCE COMPLETION

DIRECTIONS & EXAMPLE QUESTION

The following directions are to be used for all sentence completion questions:

> **Directions:** Choose the answer choice that best answers the question presented.

Below is an example sentence completion question:

Example Question

"Which one is a ride at an amusement park?"

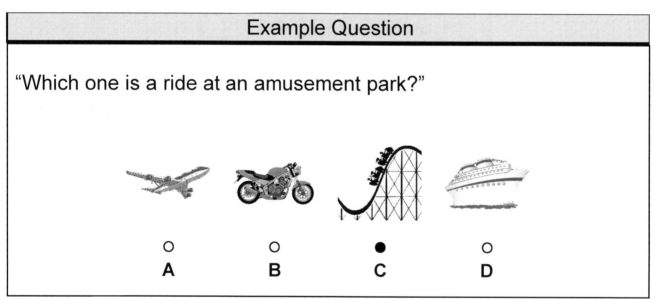

A	B	C	D
○	○	●	○

Example: A roller coaster is a ride at an amusement park. It is possible to ride the other objects shown, but they are not rides in an amusement park.

Question 1

"Which one does not provide light?"

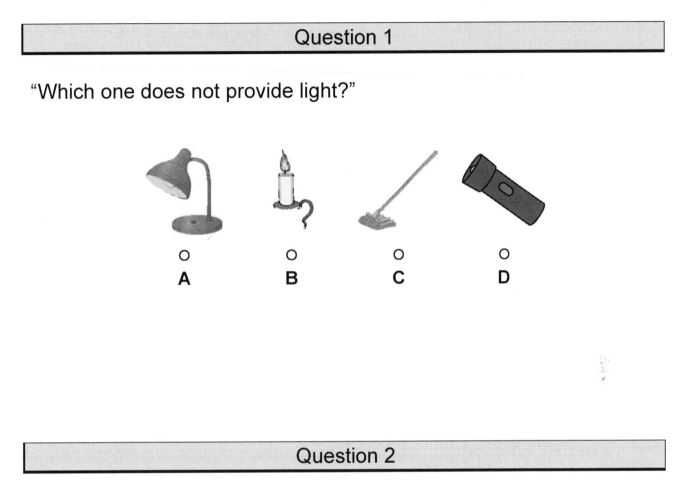

O   O   O   O
A   B   C   D

Question 2

"Which one is found on a farm?"

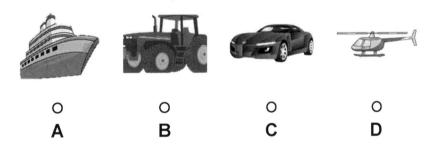

O   O   O   O
A   B   C   D

Question 3

"Which one is the hardest to roll?"

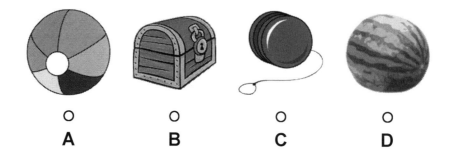

O	O	O	O
A	B	C	D

Question 4

"Which one provides oxygen?"

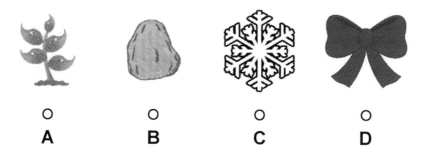

O	O	O	O
A	B	C	D

Question 5

"Which one is most like a comb?"

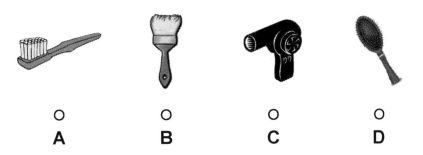

<table>
<tr><td>O</td><td>O</td><td>O</td><td>O</td></tr>
<tr><td>**A**</td><td>**B**</td><td>**C**</td><td>**D**</td></tr>
</table>

Question 6

"Which one does not always require electricity?"

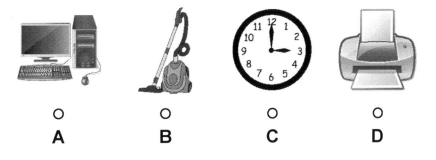

<table>
<tr><td>O</td><td>O</td><td>O</td><td>O</td></tr>
<tr><td>**A**</td><td>**B**</td><td>**C**</td><td>**D**</td></tr>
</table>

Question 7

"Which one is extinct?"

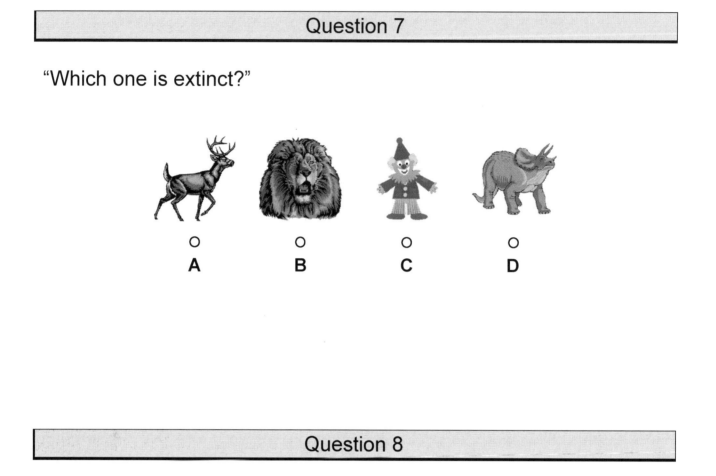

O	O	O	O
A	B	C	D

Question 8

"Which one is the most nutritious?"

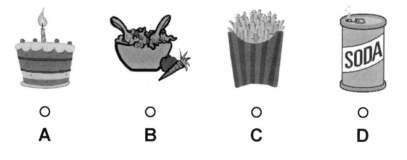

O	O	O	O
A	B	C	D

Question 9

"Which one is not used for cutting?"

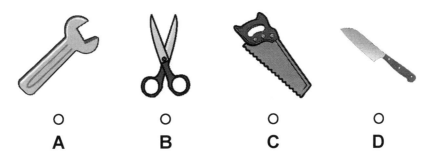

| A | B | C | D |

Question 10

"Which one is usually a lunch entrée?"

| A | B | C | D |

Question 11

"Which one belongs on an office desk?"

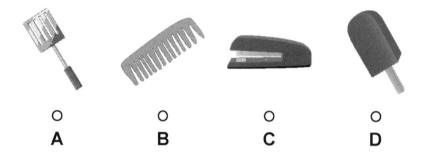

O	O	O	O
A	B	C	D

Question 12

"Which one is used for flotation?"

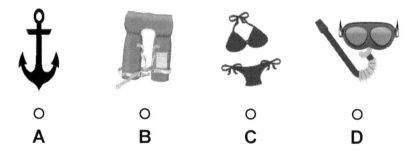

O	O	O	O
A	B	C	D

Question 13

"Which one can be found in a pond?"

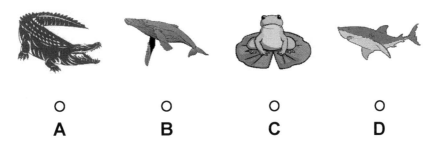

   ○   ○   ○   ○
   A   B   C   D

Question 14

"Which one is used for scooping?"

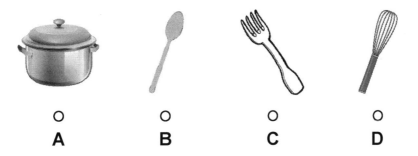

   ○   ○   ○   ○
   A   B   C   D

Question 15

"Which one does not have a shell?"

O	O	O	O
A	**B**	**C**	**D**

Question 16

"Which one is needed after a blizzard?"

O	O	O	O
A	**B**	**C**	**D**

Question 17

"Which one is a lucky charm?"

A   B   C   D

Question 18

"Which one is not used for communication?"

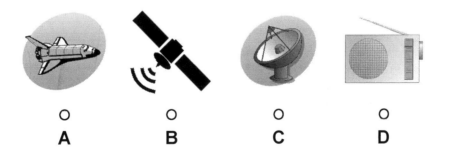

A   B   C   D

VERBAL
CLASSIFICATION

DIRECTIONS & EXAMPLE QUESTION

The following directions are to be used for all verbal classification questions:

Directions: The figures in the top row are alike in some way. Choose the figure in the bottom row that most belongs with the figures in the top row.

Below is an example verbal classification question:

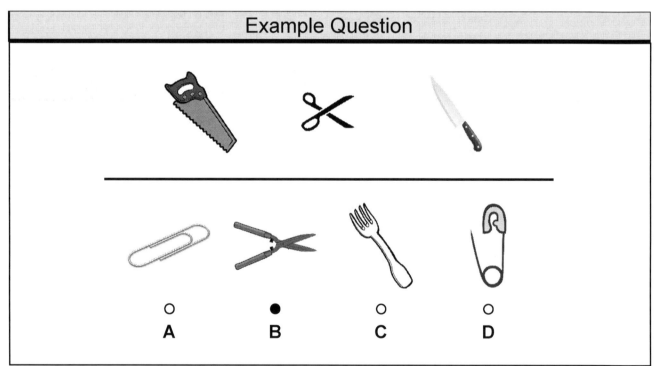

Example Question

○	●	○	○
A	B	C	D

Explanation: All of the figures in the top row are tools mainly used for cutting. Shears are also a tool used primarily for cutting, especially when gardening. Forks are not primarily used for cutting and neither are safety pins.

Question 1

O	O	O	O
A	**B**	**C**	**D**

Question 2

O	O	O	O
A	**B**	**C**	**D**

Question 3

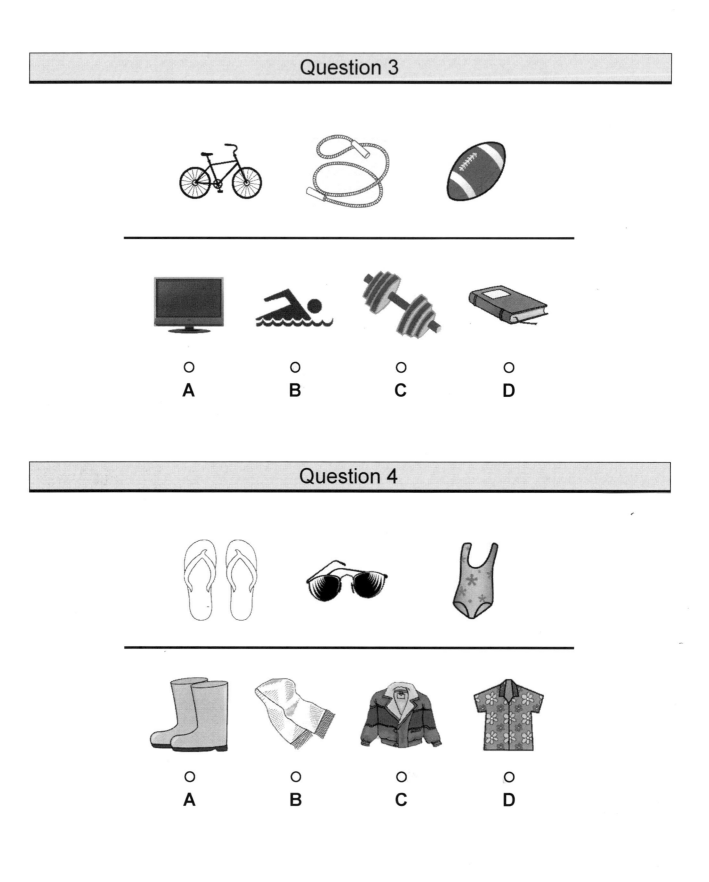

A B C D

Question 4

A B C D

Question 5

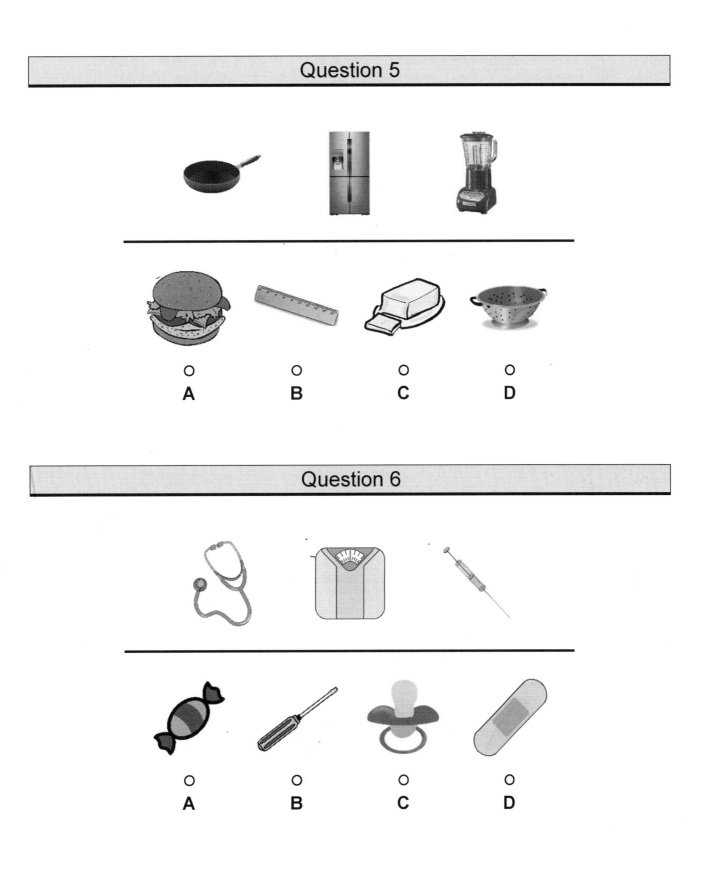

Question 7

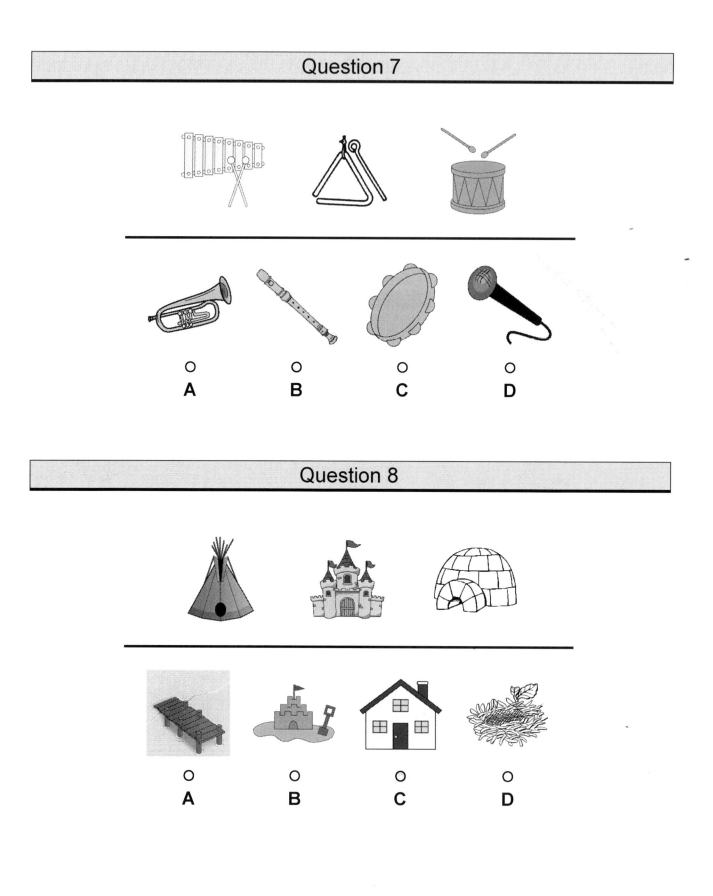

○
A

○
B

○
C

○
D

Question 8

○
A

○
B

○
C

○
D

Question 9

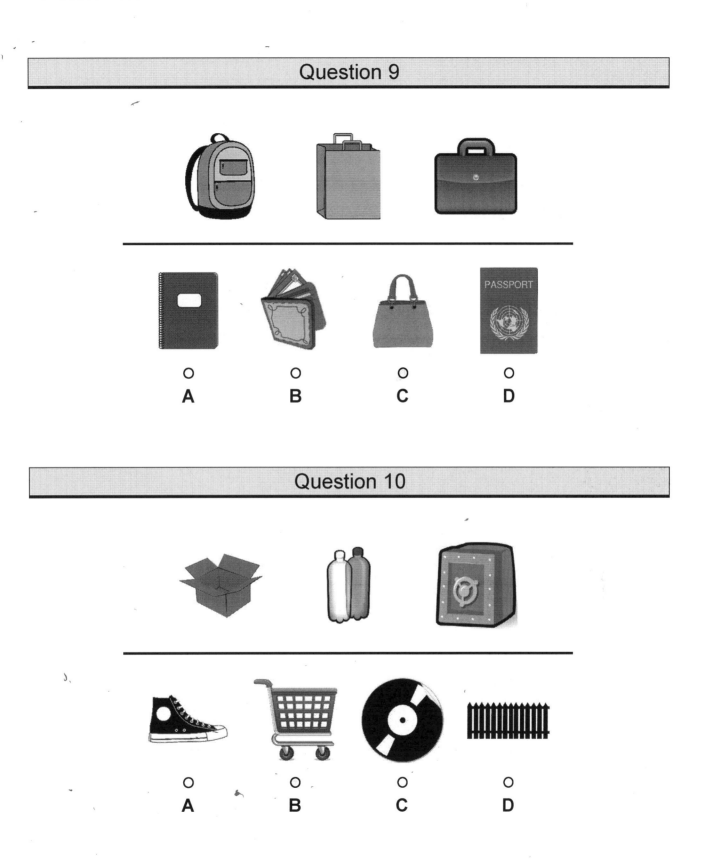

○	○	○	○
A	B	C	D

Question 10

○	○	○	○
A	B	C	D

Question 11

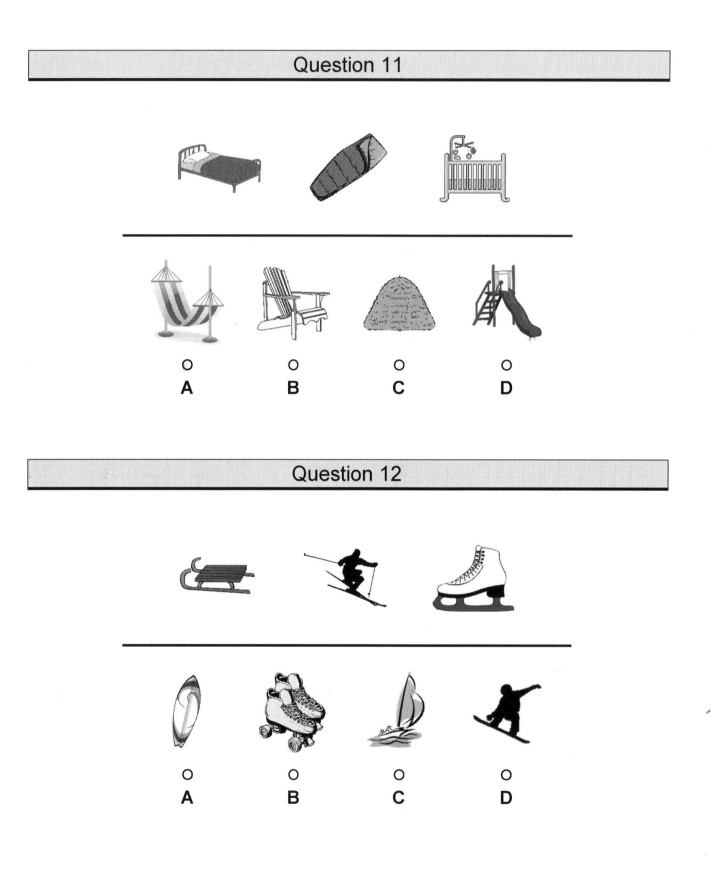

○ A   ○ B   ○ C   ○ D

Question 12

○ A   ○ B   ○ C   ○ D

Question 13

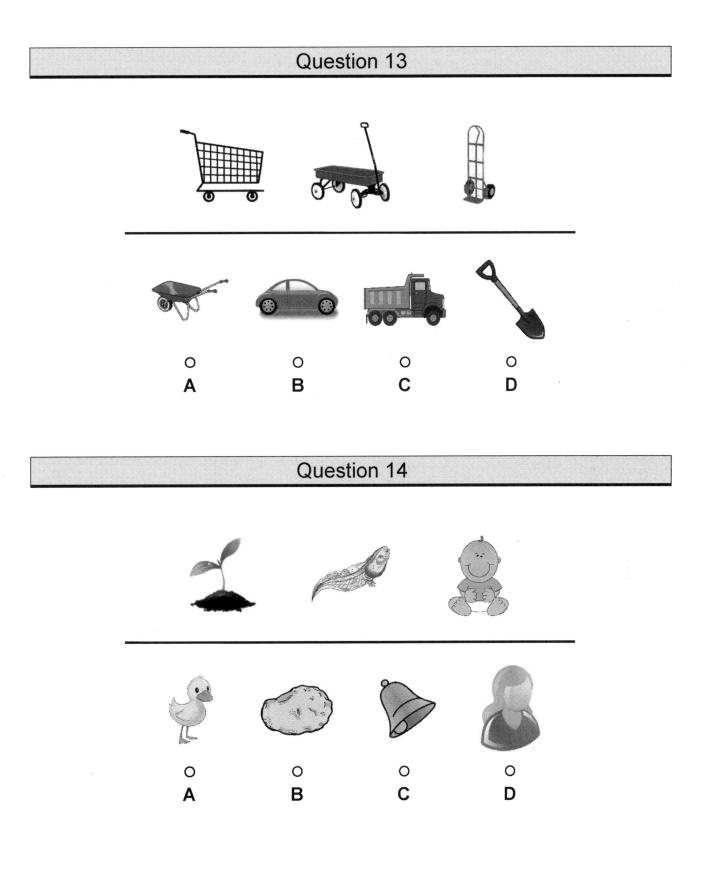

Question 14

○   ○   ○   ○
A   B   C   D

Question 15

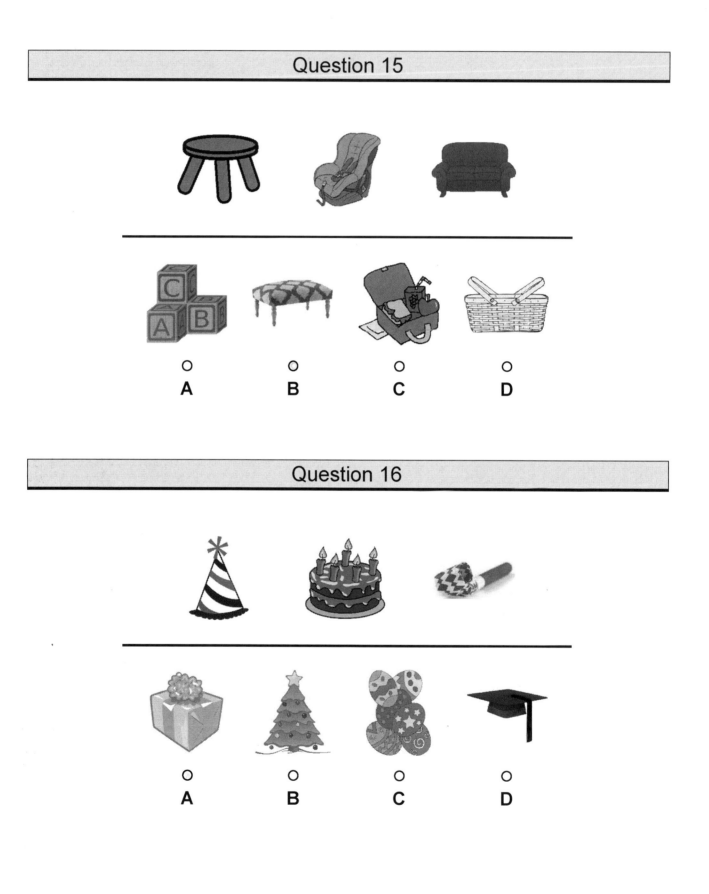

○
A

○
B

○
C

○
D

Question 16

○
A

○
B

○
C

○
D

Question 17

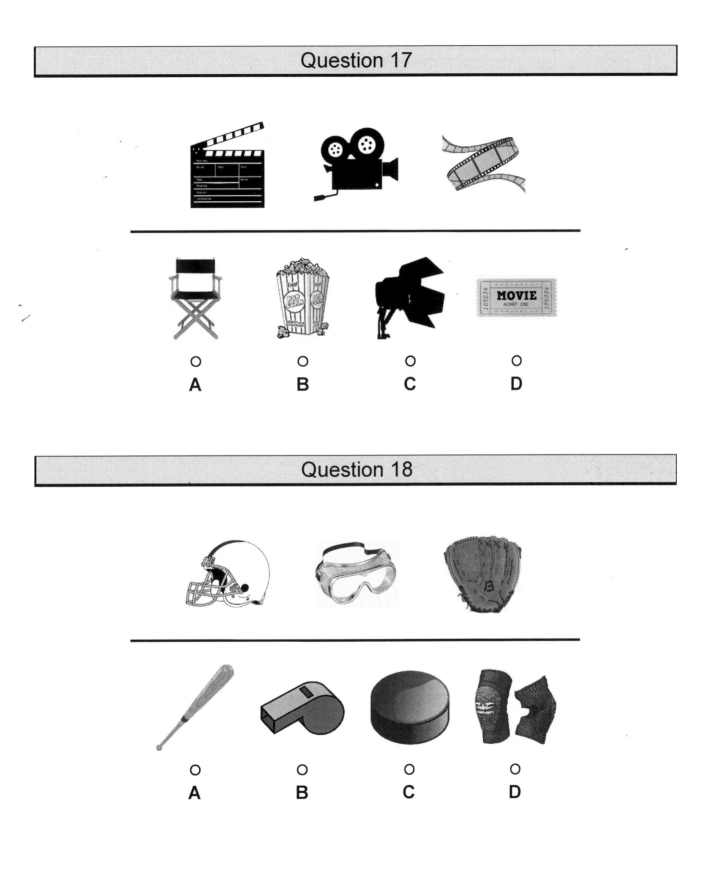

O
A

O
B

O
C

O
D

Question 18

O
A

O
B

O
C

O
D

QUANTITATIVE
Battery

NUMBER
ANALOGIES

DIRECTIONS & EXAMPLE QUESTION

The following directions are to be used for all number analogies questions:

Directions: For each question, in the grid of four squares, the top two figures are related to each other numerically. Choose the answer choice that is related to the bottom left figure in the same way numerically.

Below is an example number analogies question:

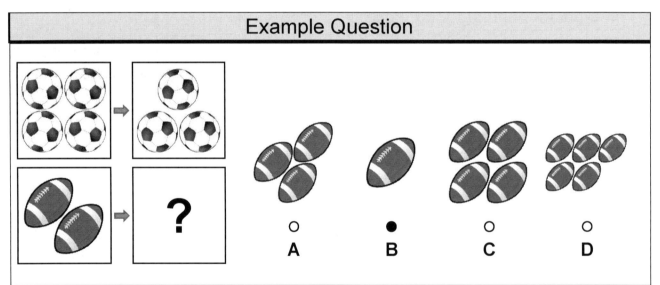

Example Question

Explanation: The first square contains 4 soccer balls. The second square contains 3, which is 1 fewer than 4. The correct answer is B because 1 fewer than 2 is 1. In other words, 2 – 1 = 1.

Question 1

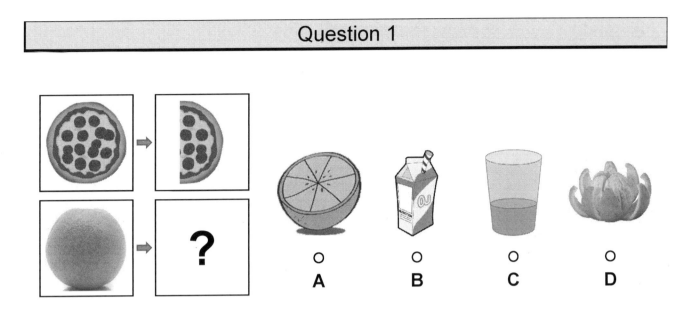

Question 2

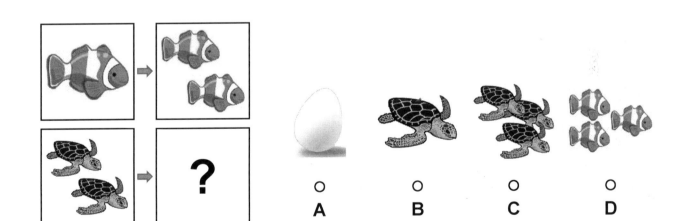

Question 3

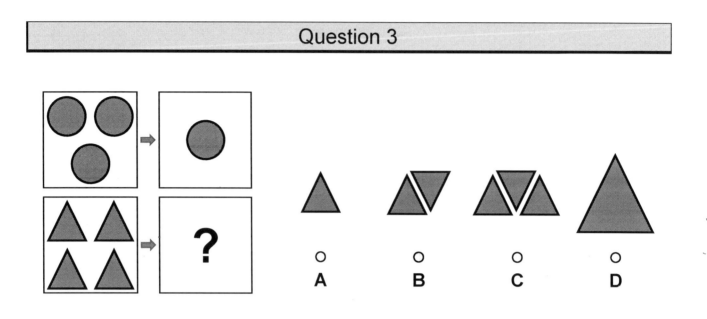

A   B   C   D

Question 4

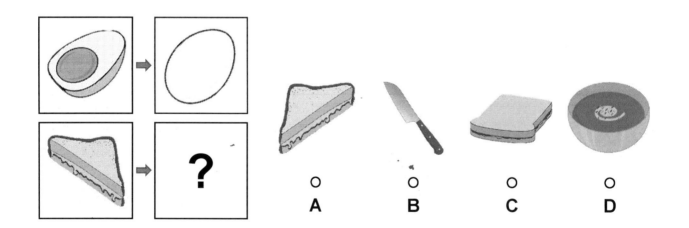

A   B   C   D

Question 5

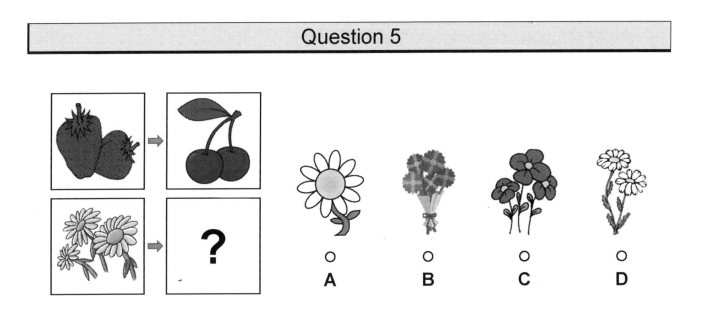

Question 6

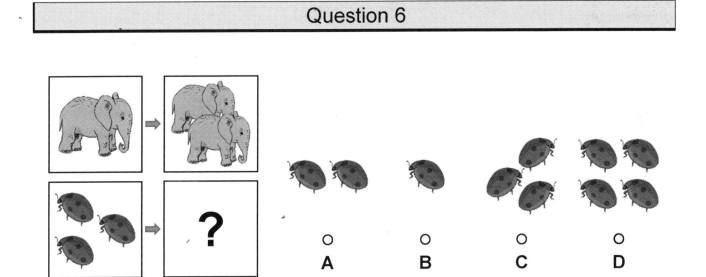

Question 7

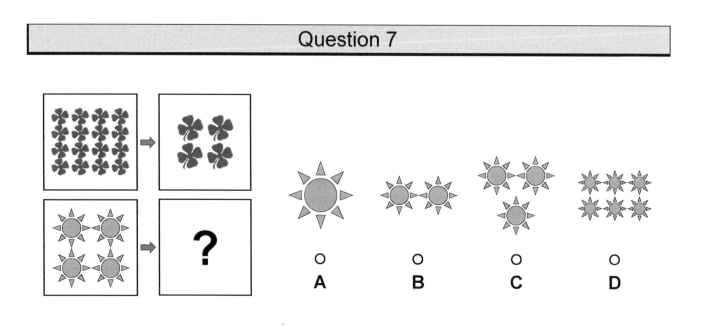

Question 8

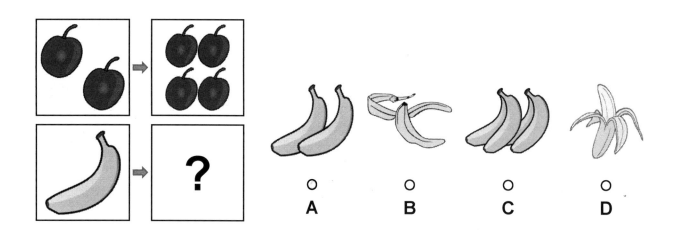

Question 9

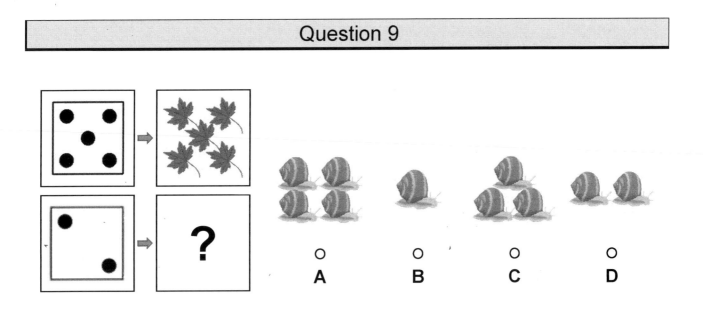

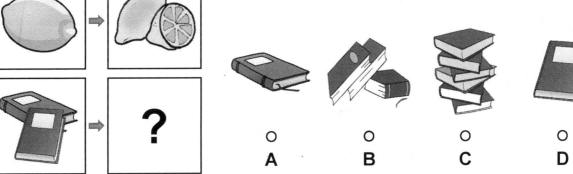

| A | B | C | D |

Question 10

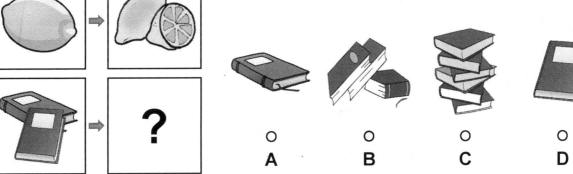

| A | B | C | D |

Question 11

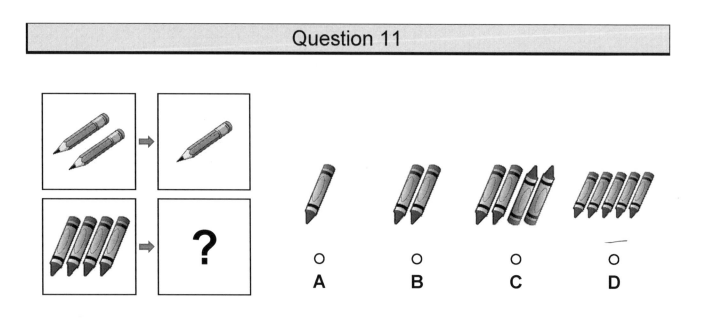

A   B   C   D

Question 12

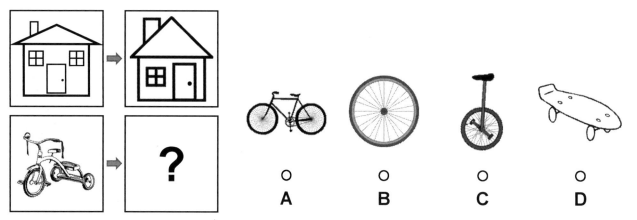

A   B   C   D

Question 13

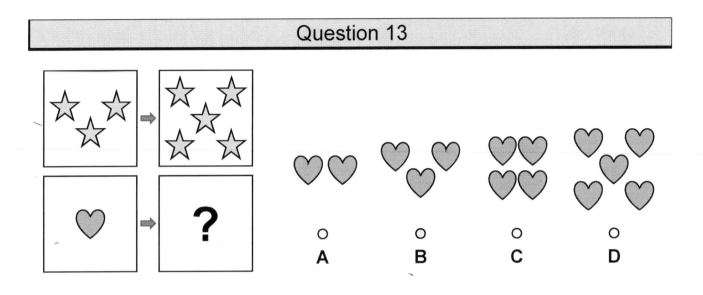

○
A

○
B

○
C

○
D

Question 14

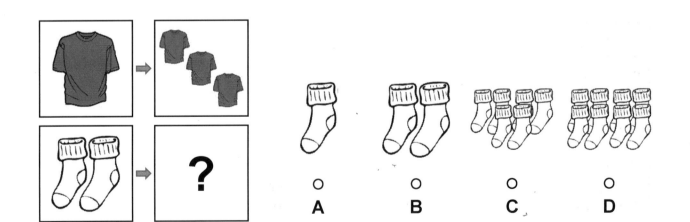

○
A

○
B

○
C

○
D

Question 15

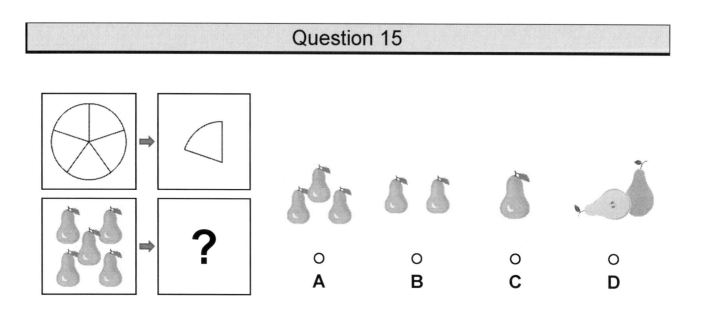

Question 16

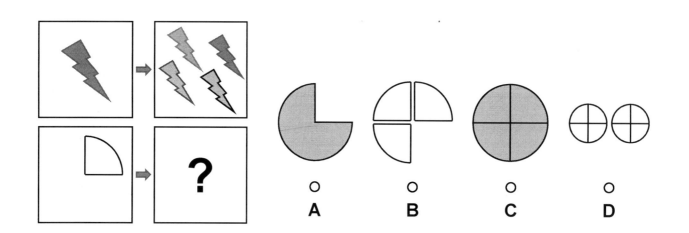

Question 17

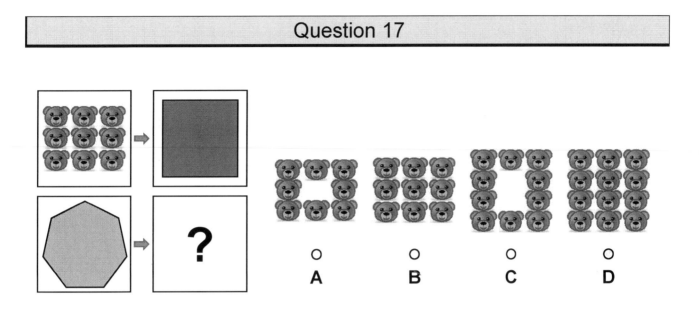

○	○
A	B

○ C   ○ D

Question 18

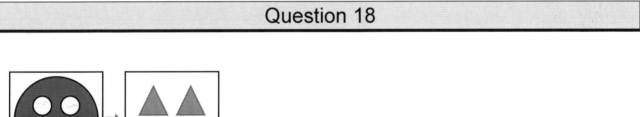

○ A   ○ B   ○ C   ○ D

NUMBER PUZZLES

DIRECTIONS & EXAMPLE QUESTION

The following directions are to be used for all number puzzles questions:

Directions: The first train has a certain number of objects. Choose the answer choice that would give the second train the same total number of objects as the first train has.

Below is an example number puzzles question:

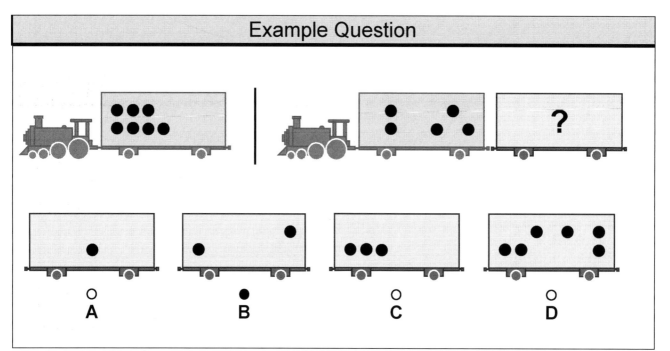

Explanation: The first train contains 7 objects. The second train contains 5 objects. It needs 2 more objects (7 – 5 = 2 or 5 + 2 = 7) in order to have the same number of objects as the first train does.

Question 1

Question 2

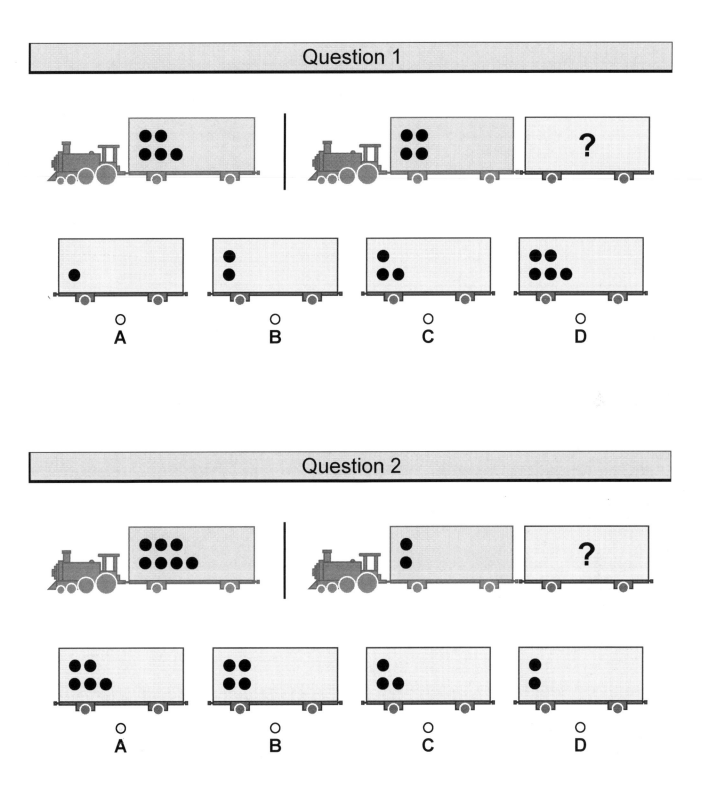

Question 3

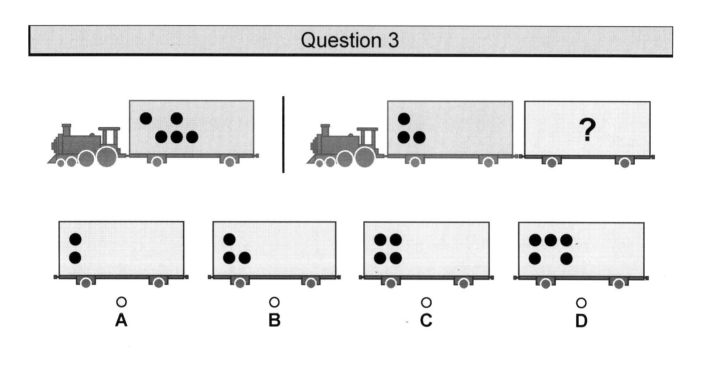

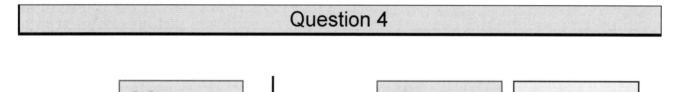

Question 4

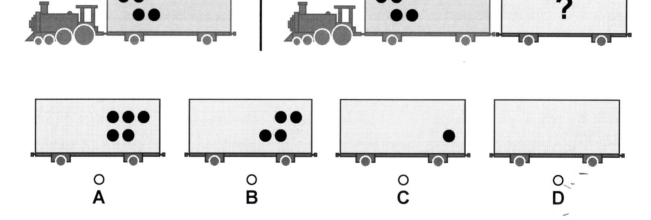

Question 5

Question 6

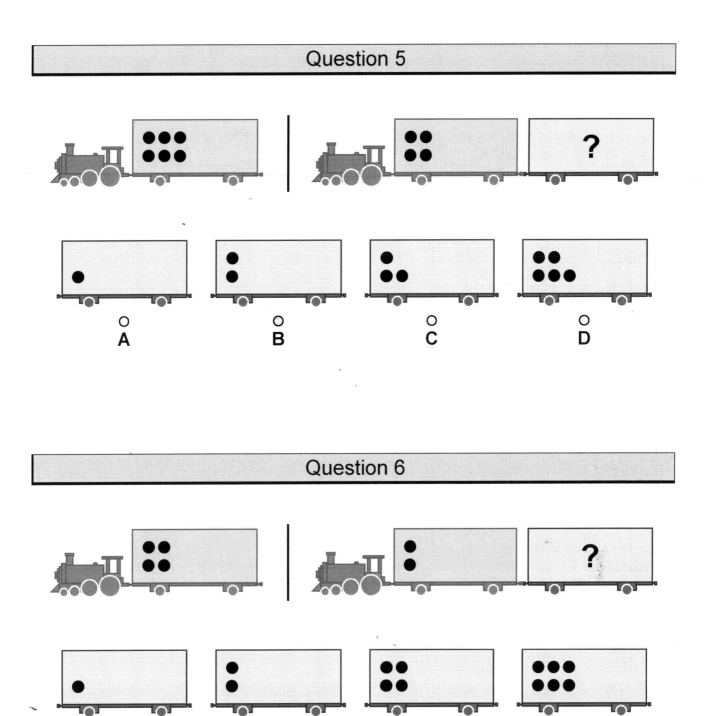

Question 7

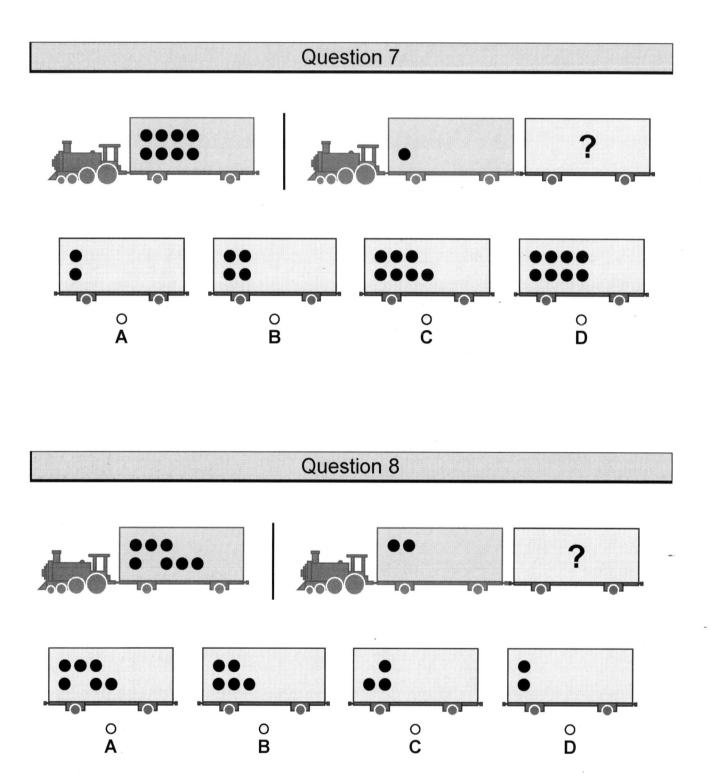

Question 8

Question 9

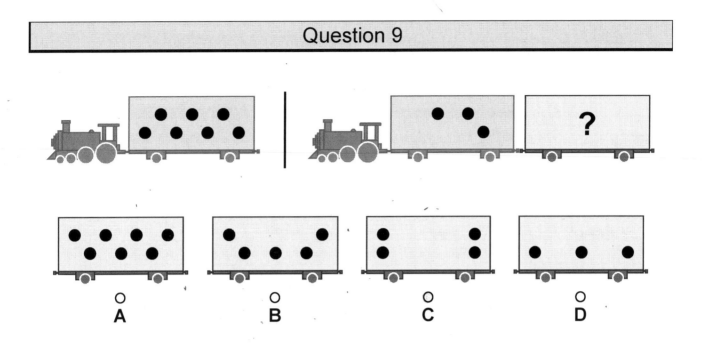

Question 10

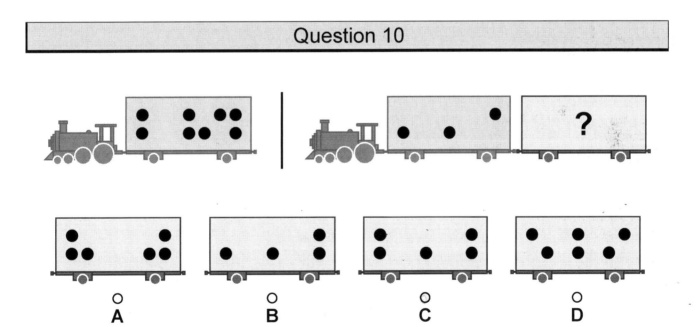

Question 11

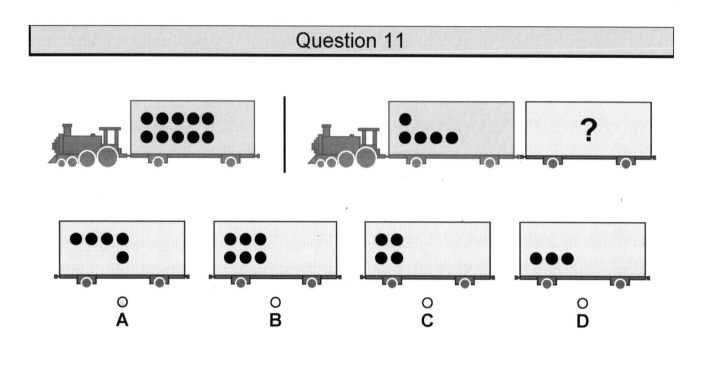

Question 12

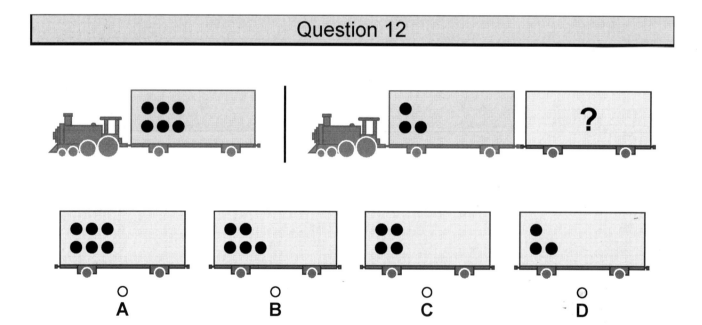

Question 13

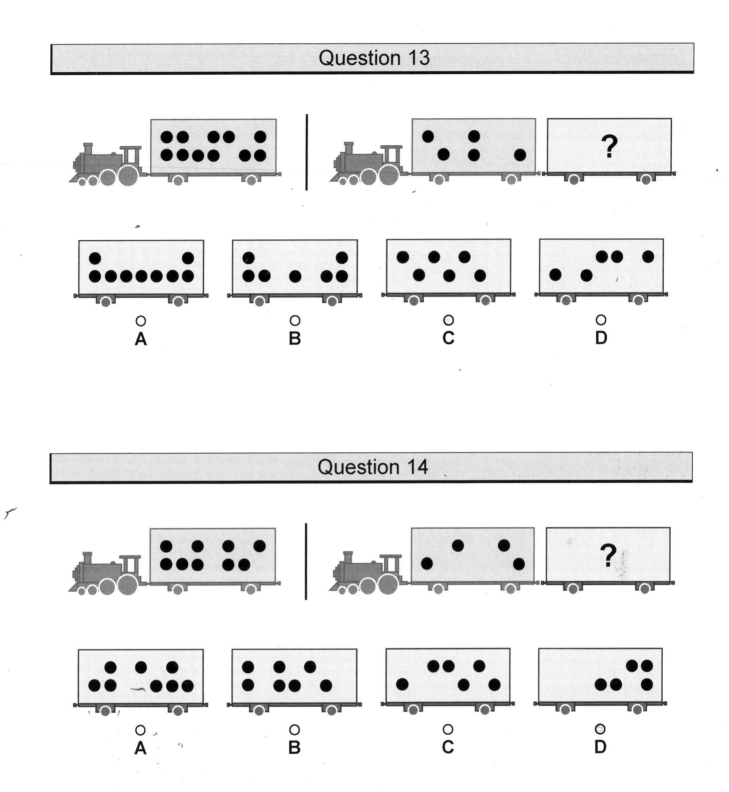

NUMBER
SERIES

DIRECTIONS & EXAMPLE QUESTION

The following directions are to be used for all number series questions:

Directions: In each question, an abacus is shown. The numbers of beads in the rows of the abacus form a pattern. Choose the answer choice that best continues the pattern in the next column of beads.

Below is an example number series question:

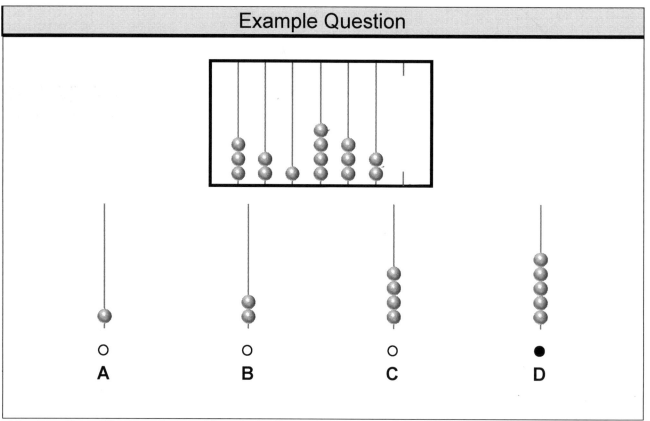

Explanation: The numbers of beads in the columns are: 3, 2, 1, 4, 3, 2. The next number should be 5, which is represented by D, because the next three numbers in the pattern are 5, 4, 3.

Question 1

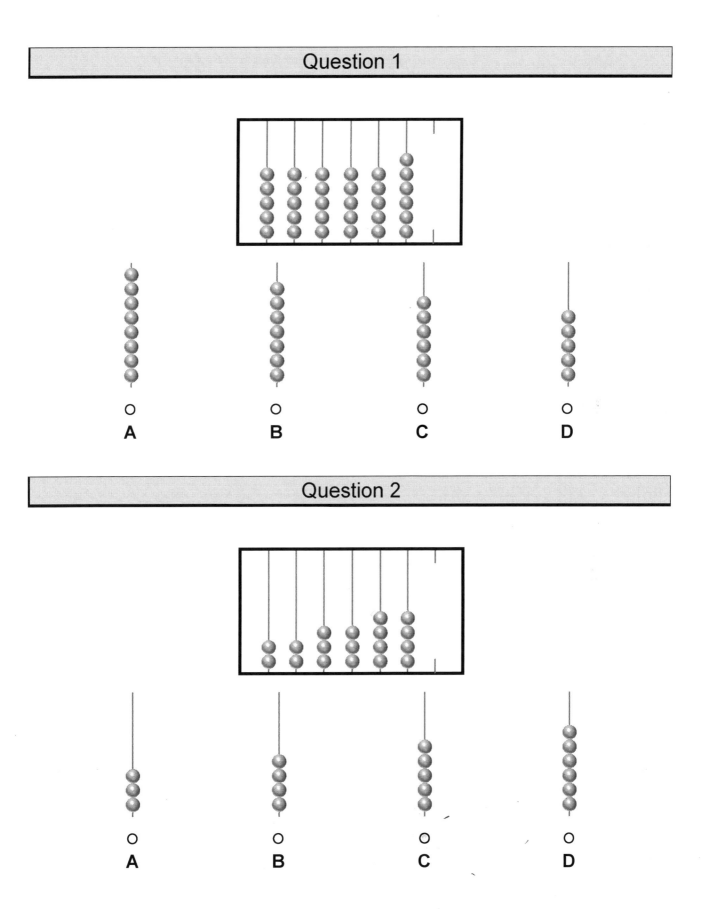

Question 2

Question 3

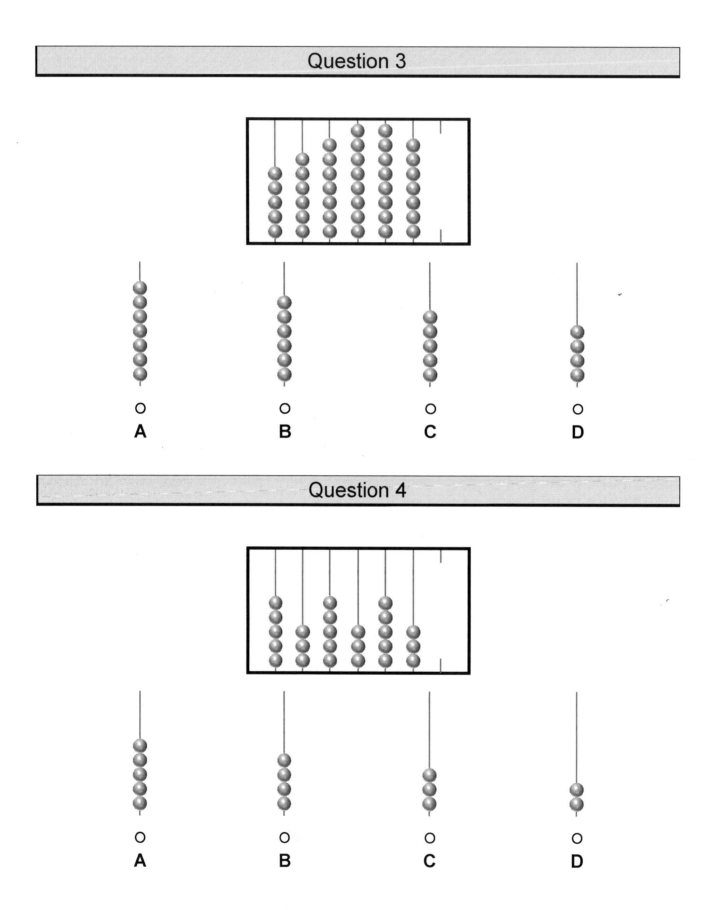

Question 4

Question 5

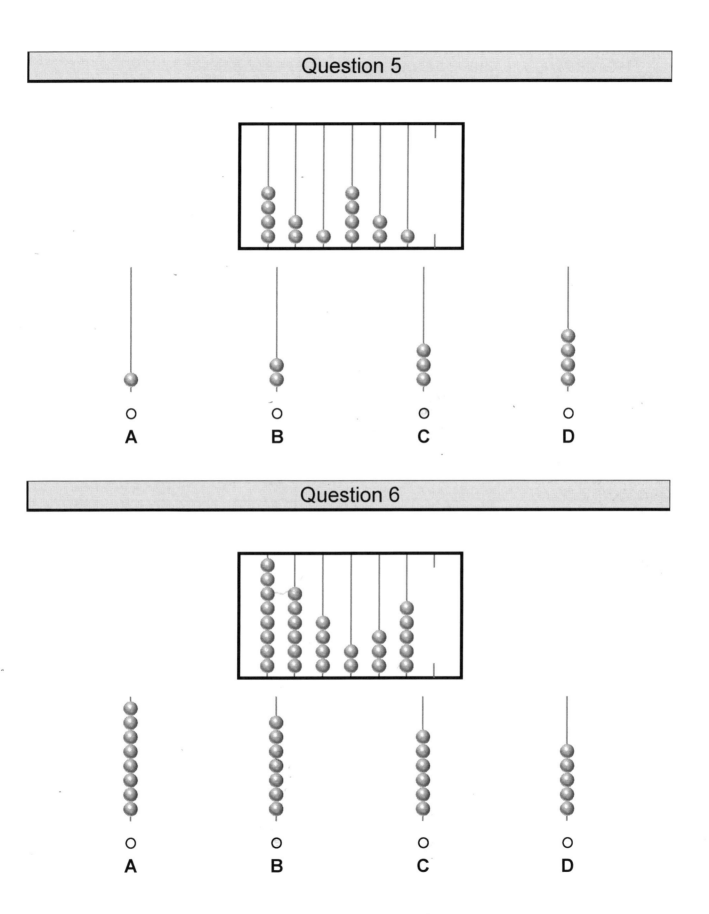

Question 6

Question 7

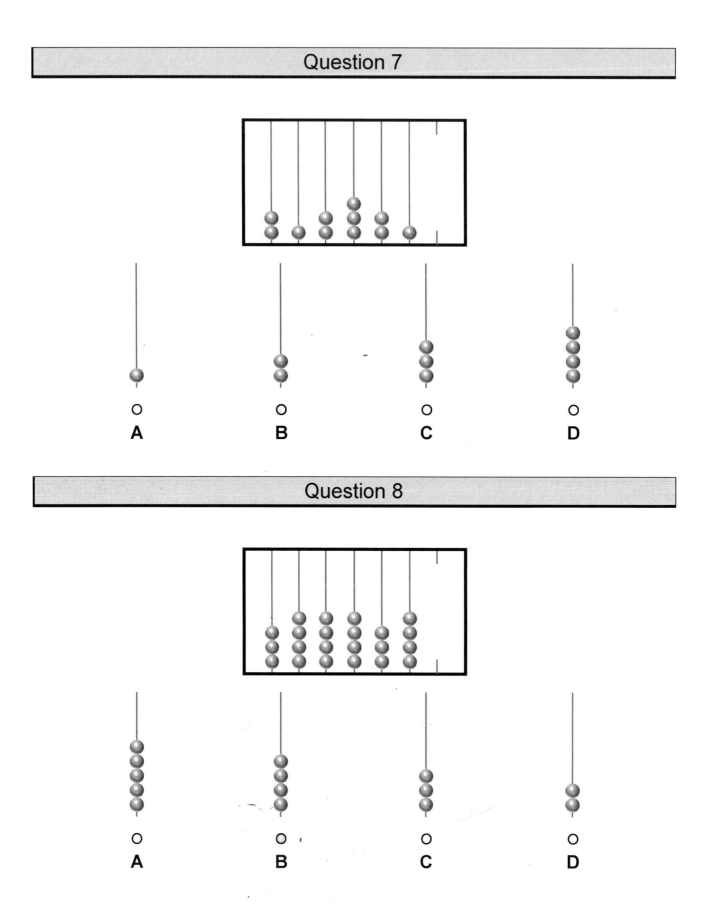

Question 8

Question 9

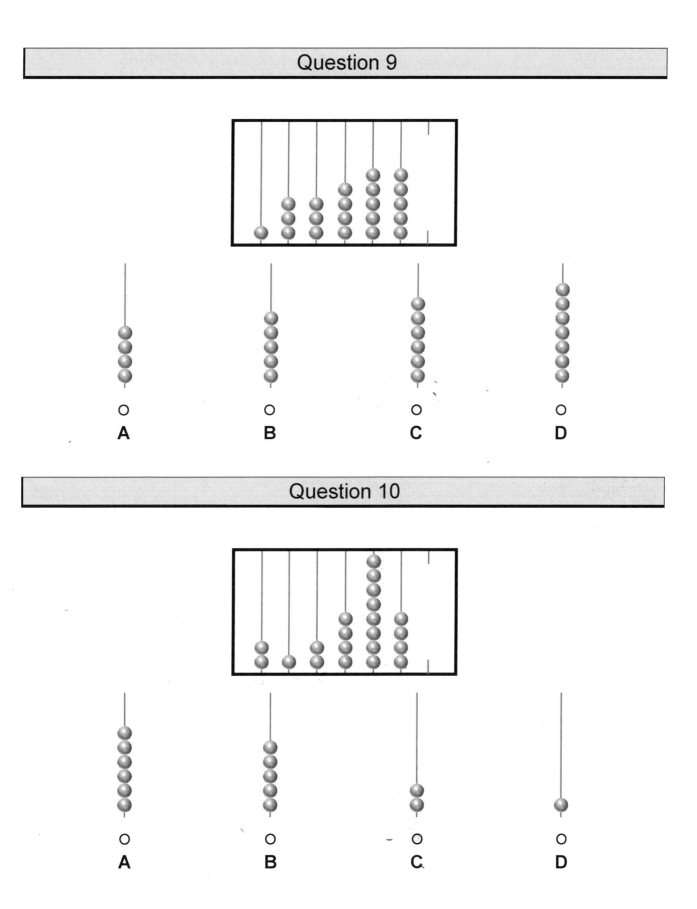

A

B

C

D

Question 10

A

B

C.

D

Question 11

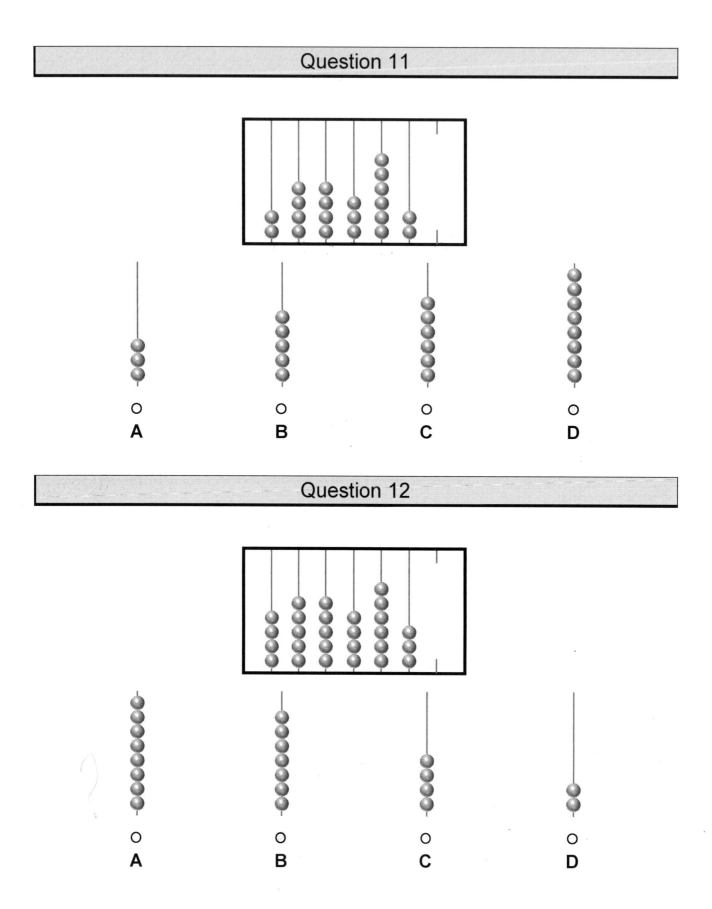

Question 12

Question 13

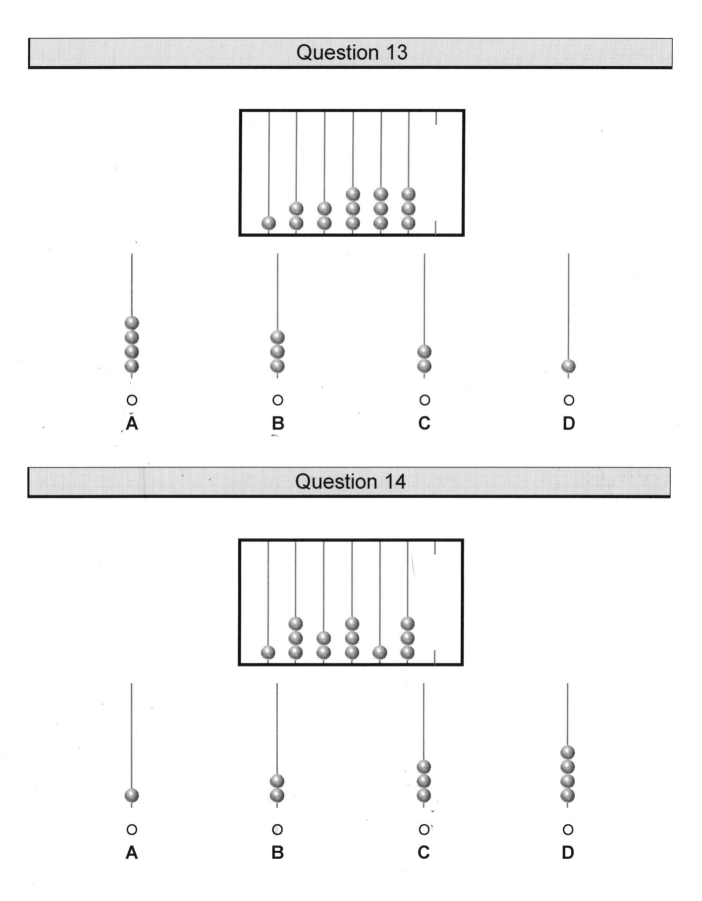

A   B   C   D

Question 14

A   B   C   D

Question 15

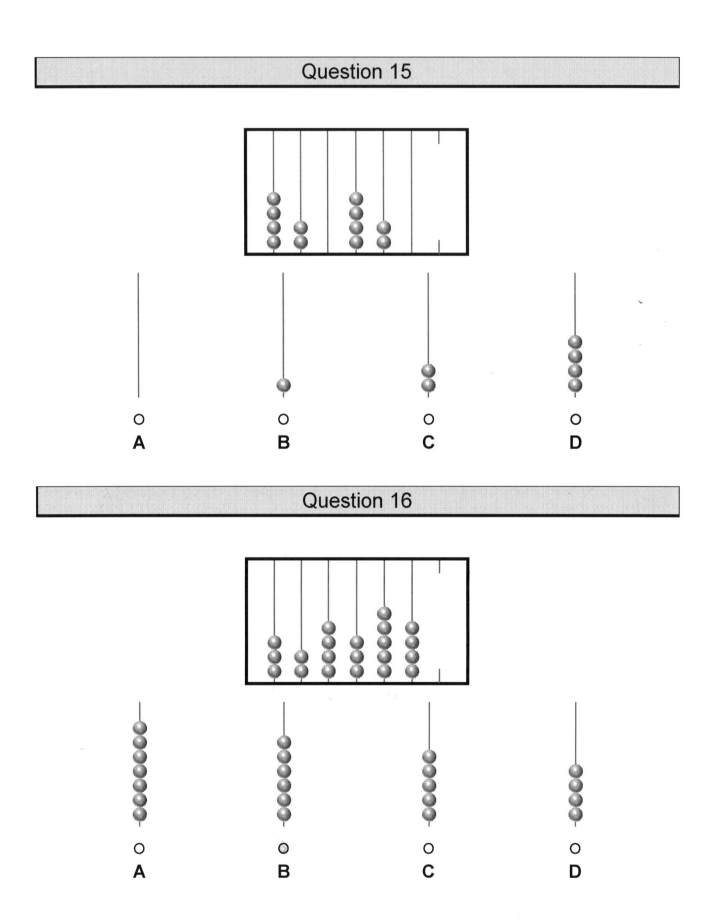

Question 16

Question 17

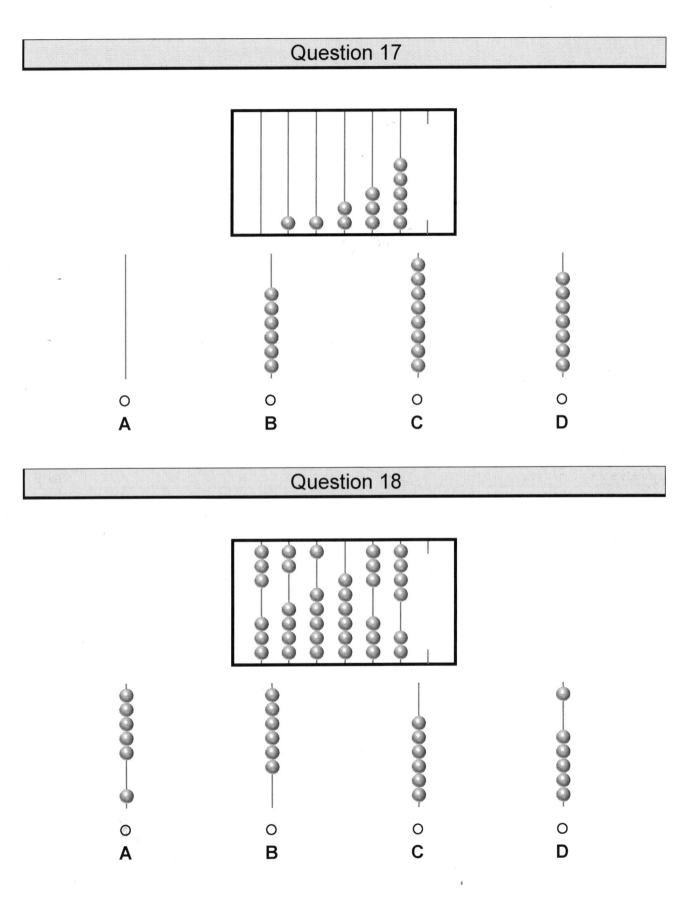

A   B   C   D

Question 18

A   B   C   D

NONVERBAL
Battery

FIGURE
MATRICES

DIRECTIONS & EXAMPLE QUESTION

The following directions are to be used for all figure matrices questions:

Directions: For each question, in the grid of four squares, the top two figures go together. Choose the answer choice that goes with the bottom left figure.

Below is an example figure matrices question:

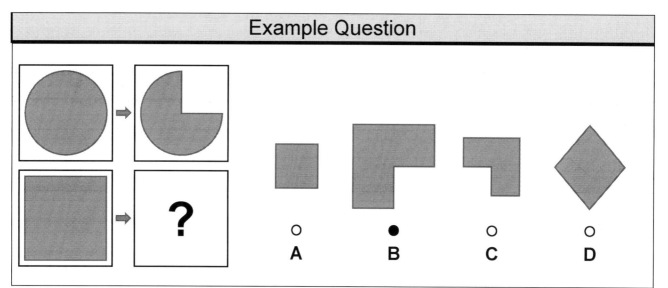

Explanation: The top two figures are related in that the top right figure is the same as the top left figure but with a quarter of the figure removed. The answer choice B is the same as the bottom left figure except with a quarter of the square removed. C is not correct because it is not the same size as the bottom left figure.

Question 1

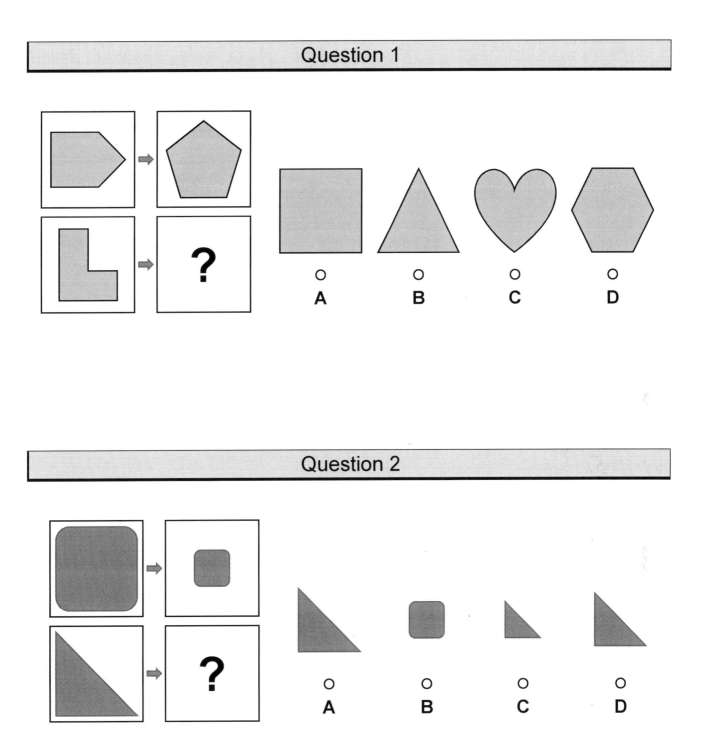

Question 2

Question 3

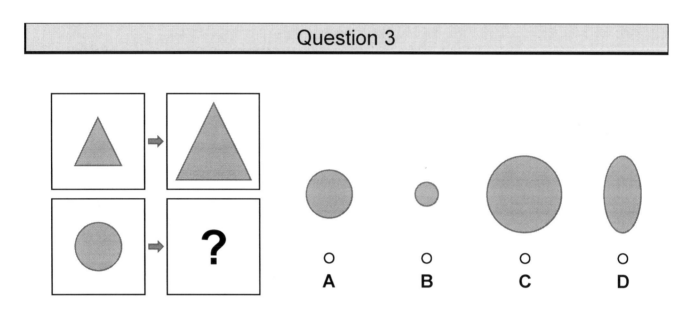

Question 4

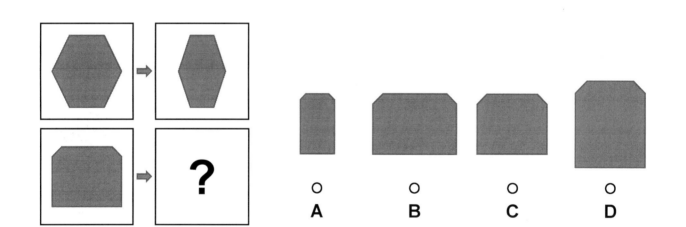

Question 5

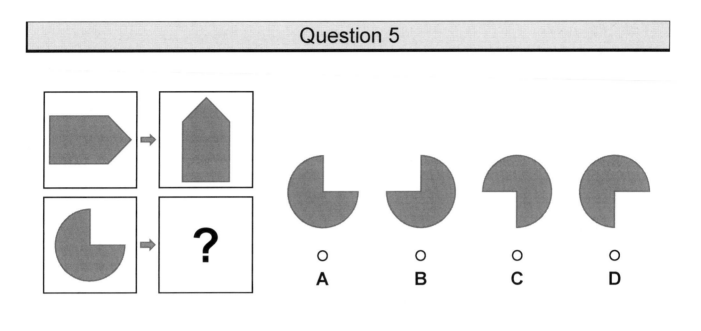

Question 6

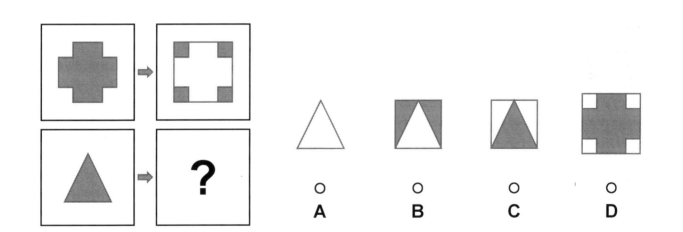

Question 7

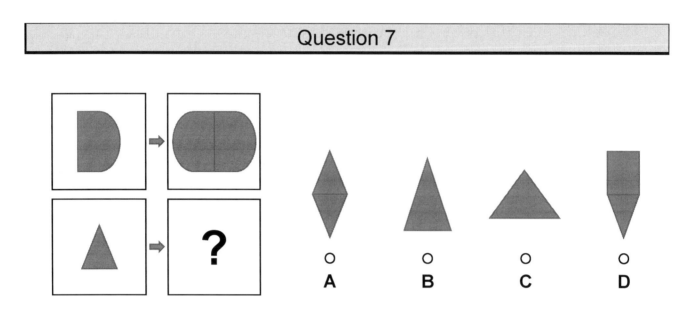

Question 8

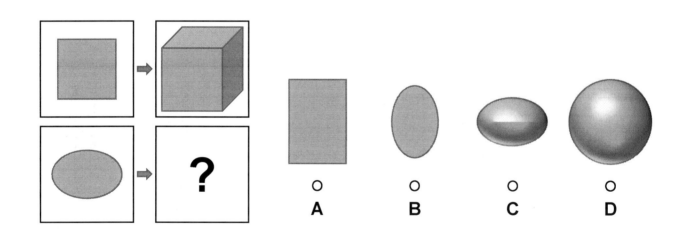

Question 9

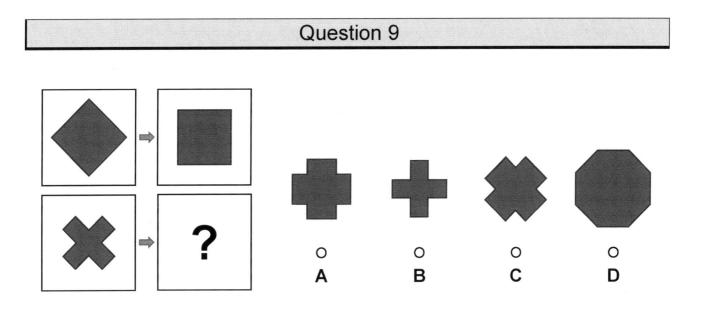

Question 10

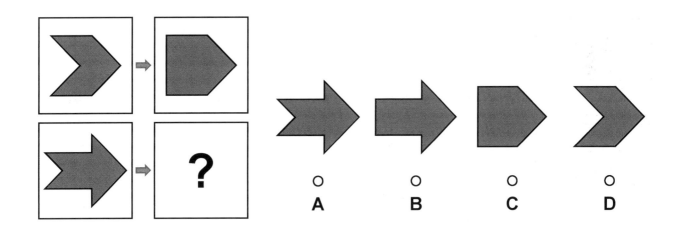

Question 11

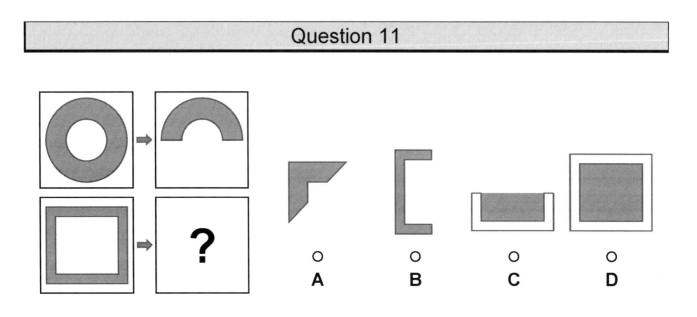

Question 12

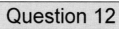

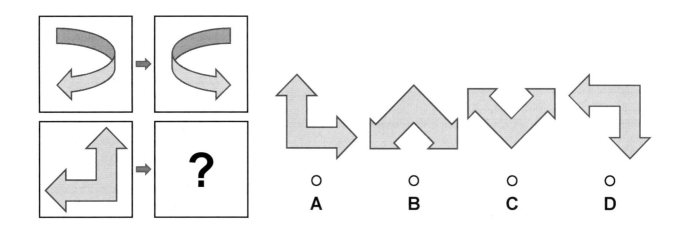

Question 13

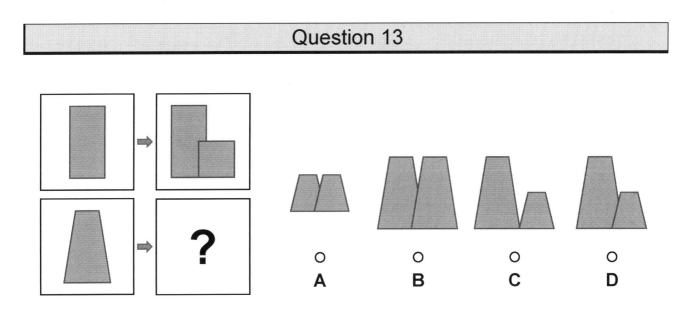

Question 14

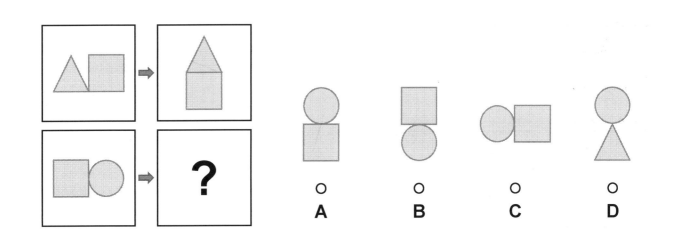

Question 15

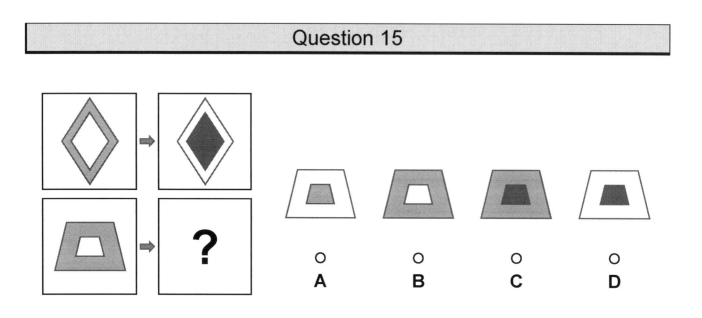

Question 16

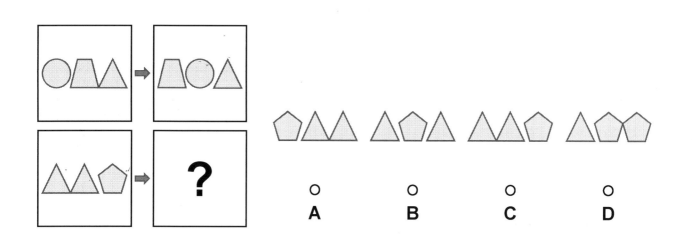

Question 17

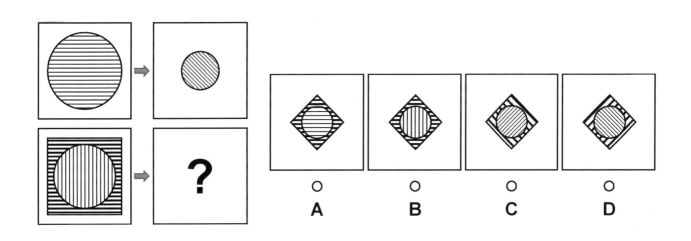

Question 18

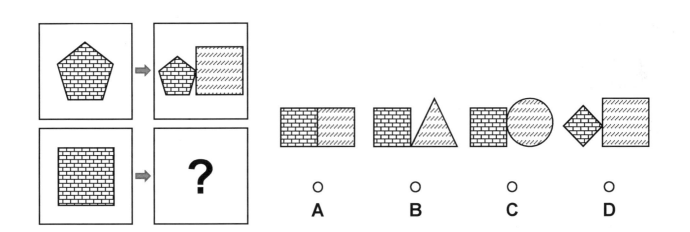

PAPER
FOLDING

DIRECTIONS & EXAMPLE QUESTION

The following directions are to be used for all paper folding questions:

Directions: In each question, a square piece of paper is folded. After it is folded all the way, holes are punched into the paper. You must figure out what the paper will look like when it is completely unfolded.

Below is an example paper folding question:

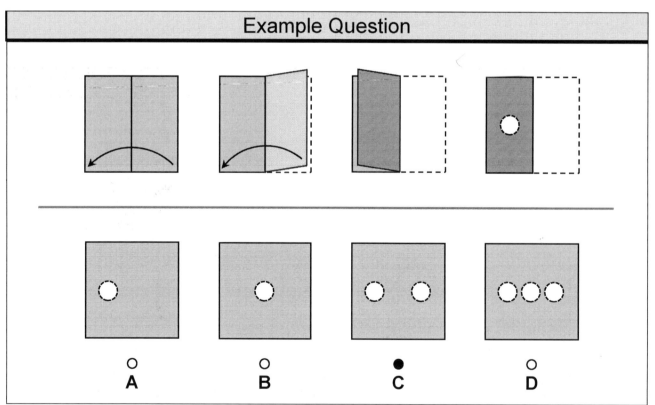

Explanation: The right side of the paper is folded over once to the left side and then a hole is punched in. Because there is only one fold, the paper will have two holes when it is completely unfolded. Thus, C must be the correct answer.

Question 1

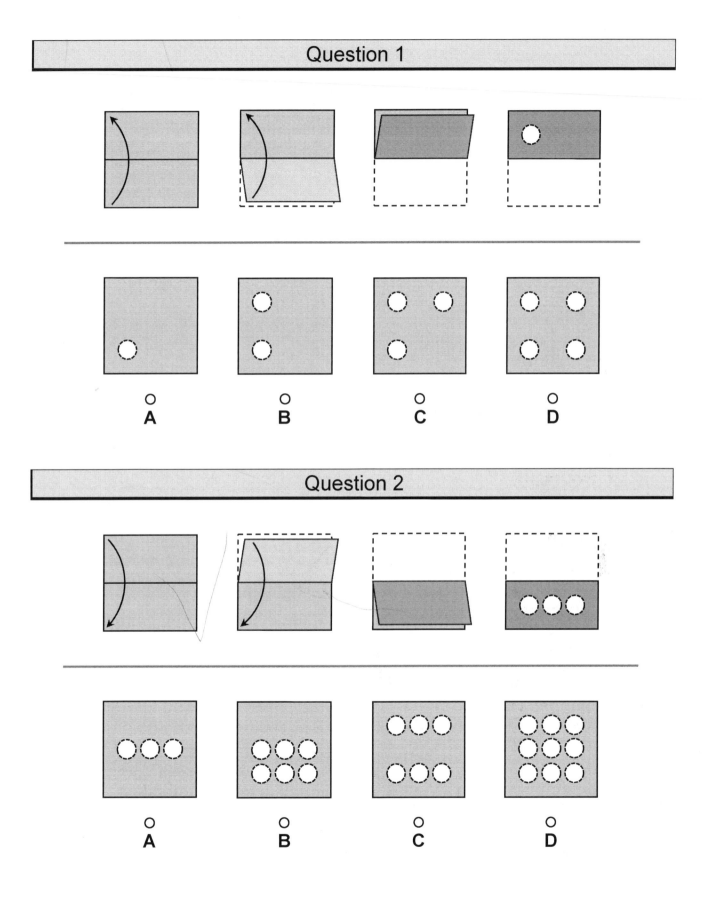

O
A

O
B

O
C

O
D

Question 2

O
A

O
B

O
C

O
D

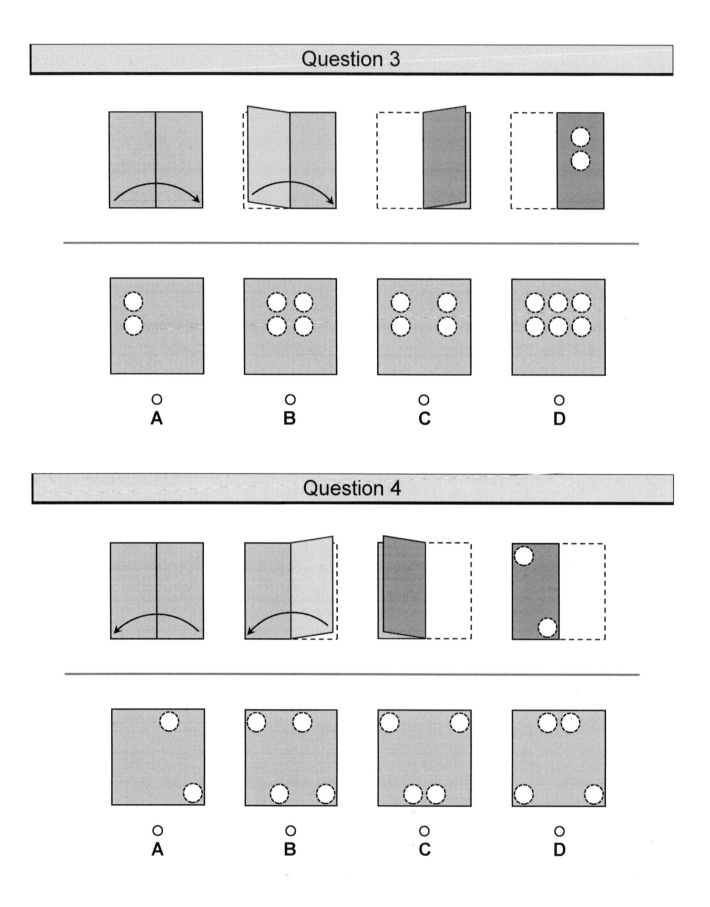

Question 5

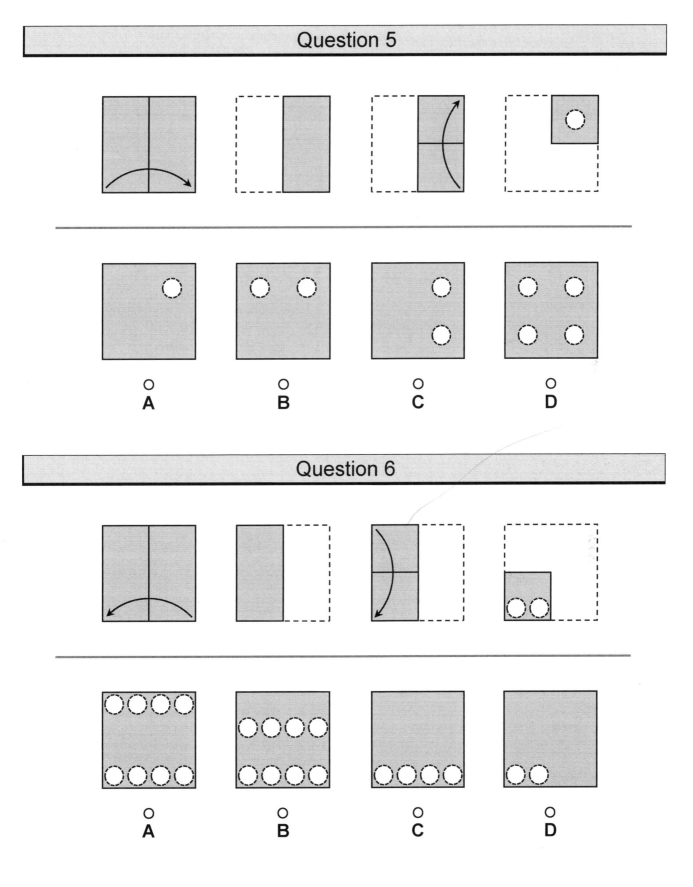

O
A

O
B

O
C

O
D

Question 6

O
A

O
B

O
C

O
D

Question 7

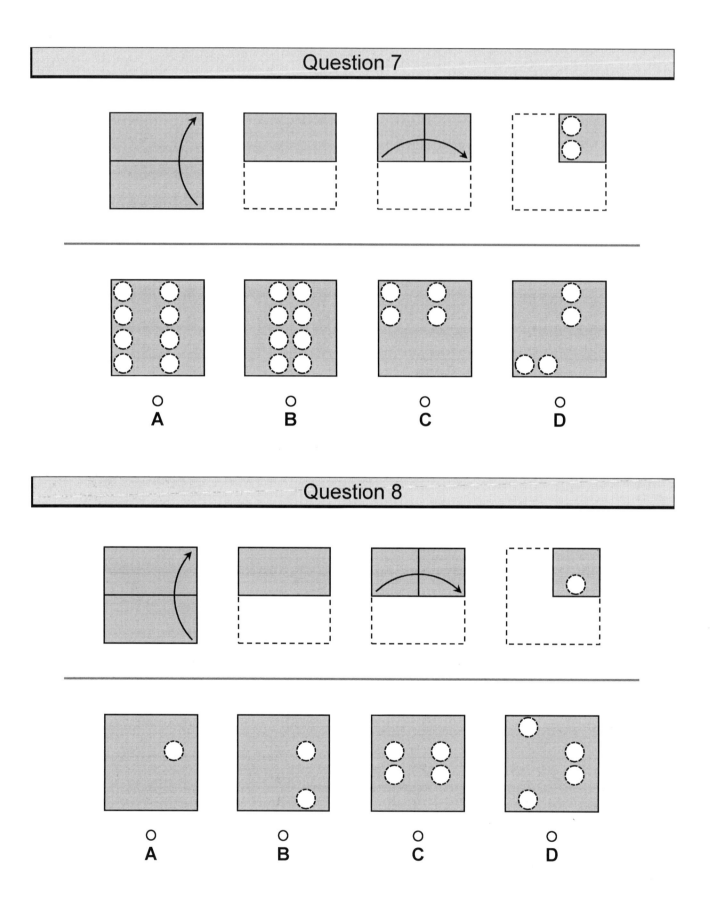

A   B   C   D

Question 8

A   B   C   D

Question 9

Question 10

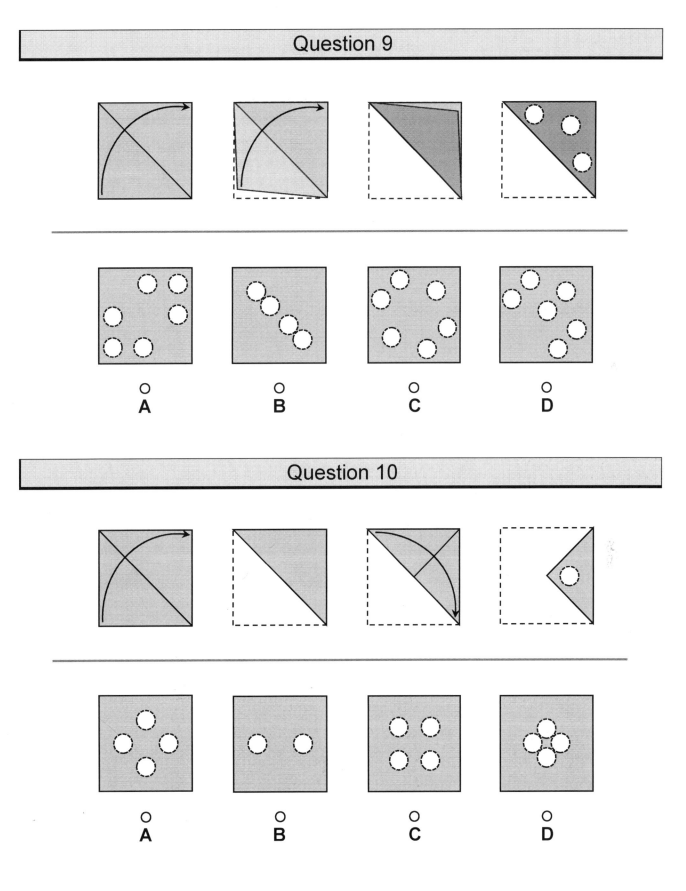

Question 11

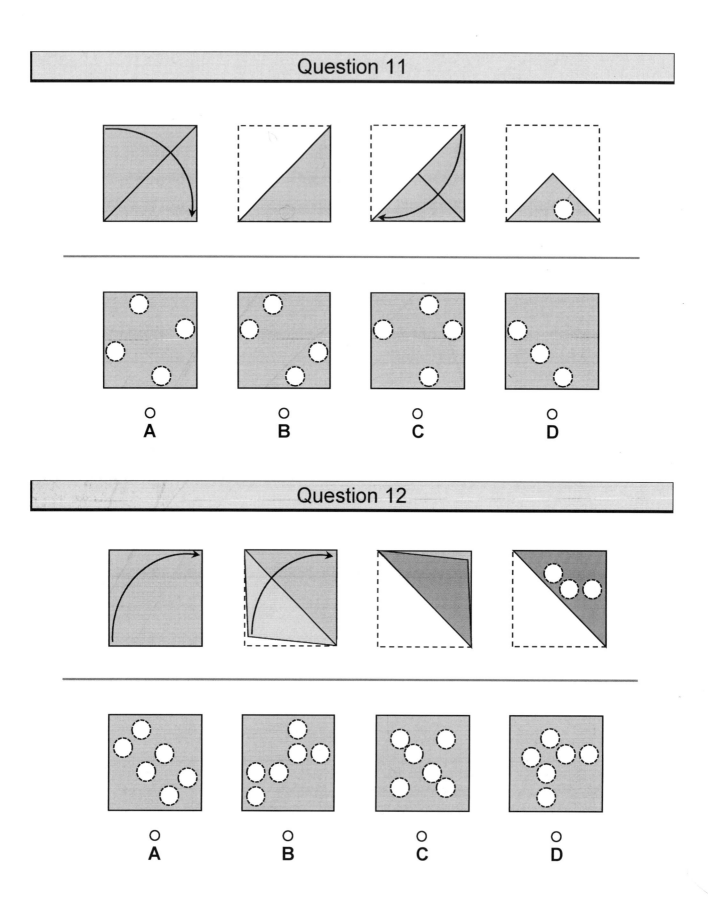

Question 12

A   B   C   D

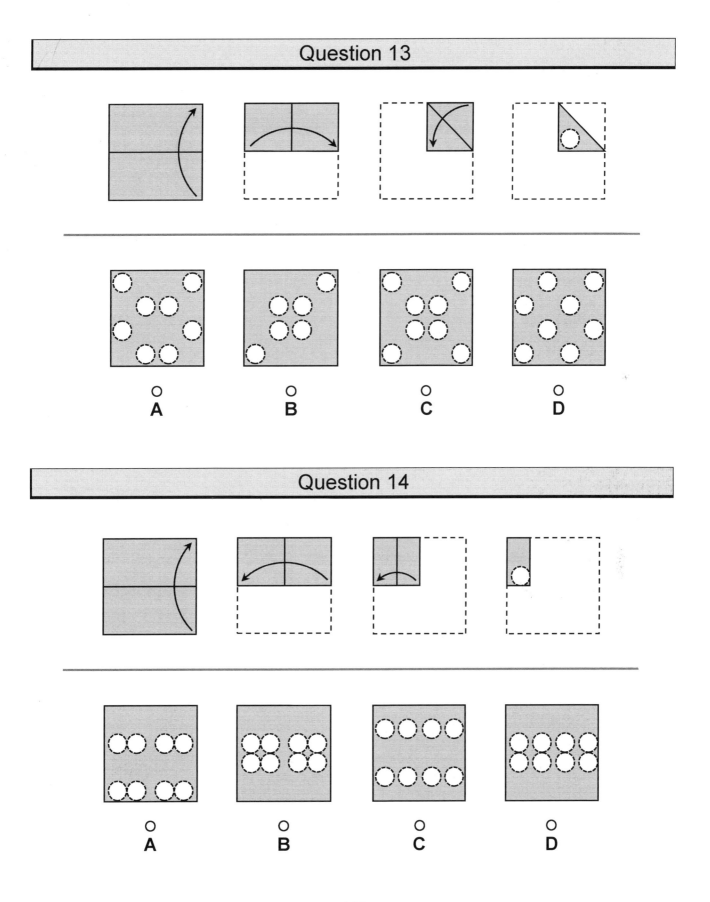

FIGURE
CLASSIFICATION

DIRECTIONS & EXAMPLE QUESTION

The following directions are to be used for all figure classification questions:

Directions: In each question, the first three figures in the top row are alike in one or more ways. Choose the figure from the bottom row that most belongs with the figures in the top row.

Below is an example figure classification question:

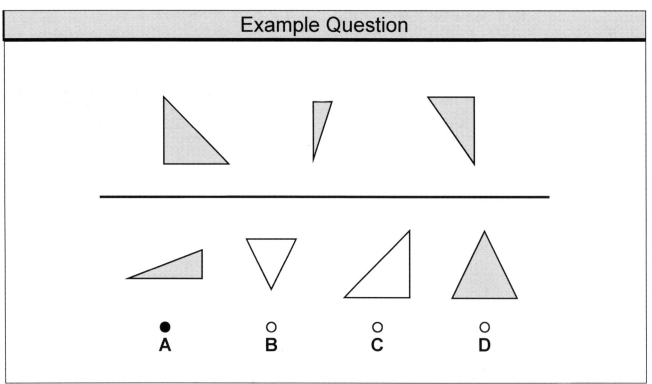

Explanation: All three of the figures in the top row are shaded and have a right angle, meaning two sides meet perpendicularly, as if to form a corner of a rectangle. Thus, A is correct. C is not correct because it is not shaded. D is not correct because it does not have a right angle.

Question 1

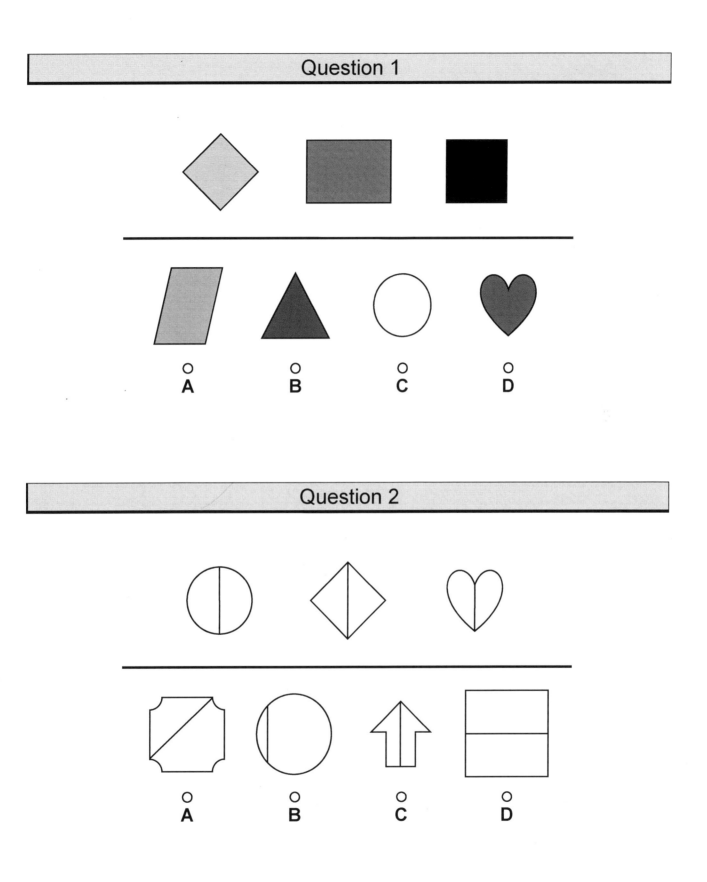

A B C D

Question 2

A B C D

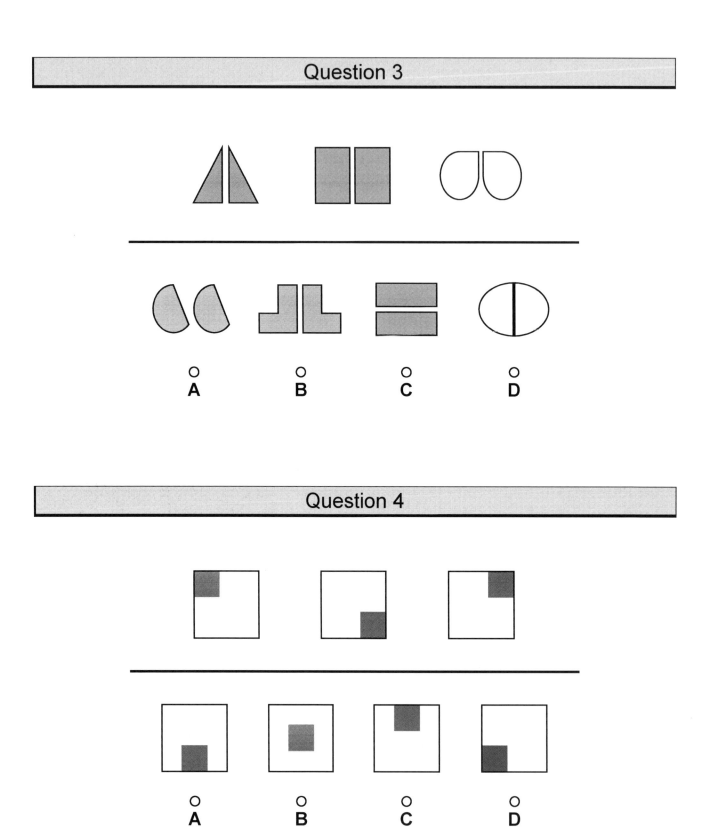

Question 3

Question 4

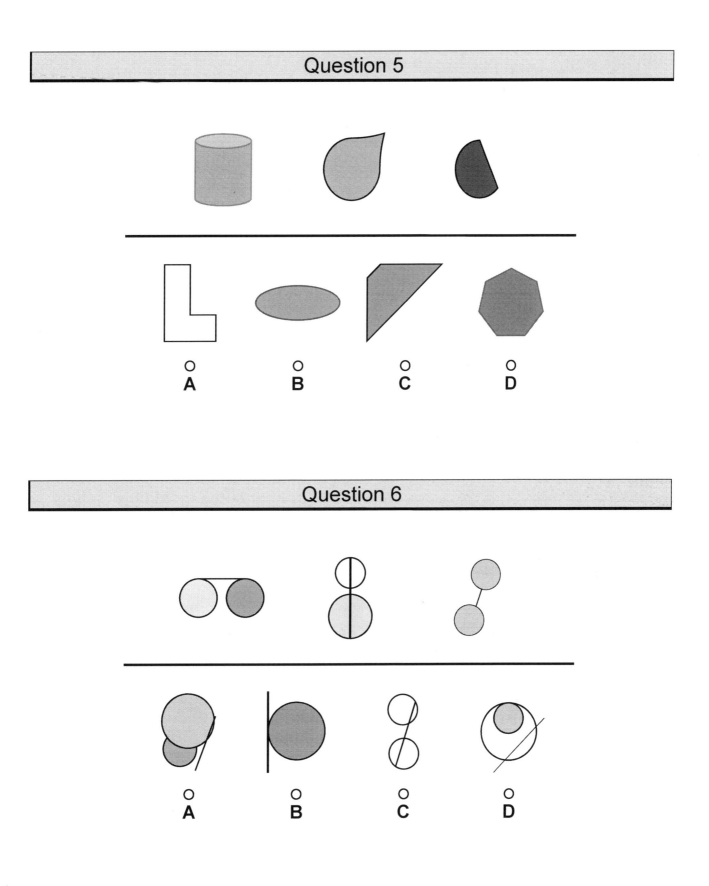

Question 5

Question 6

Question 7

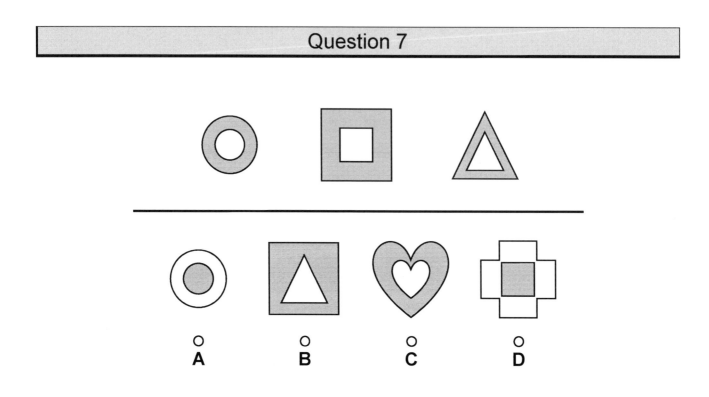

Question 8

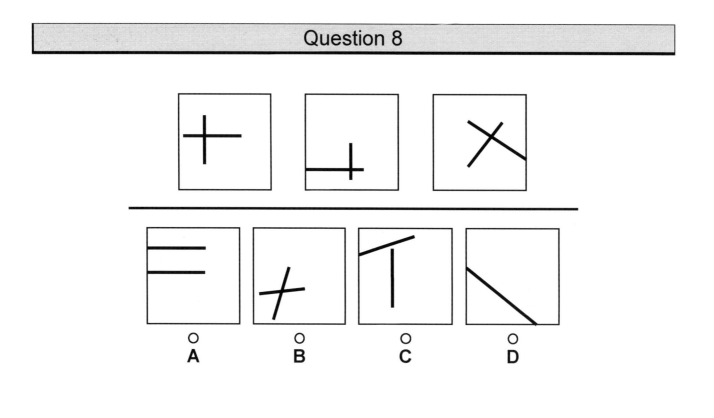

Question 9

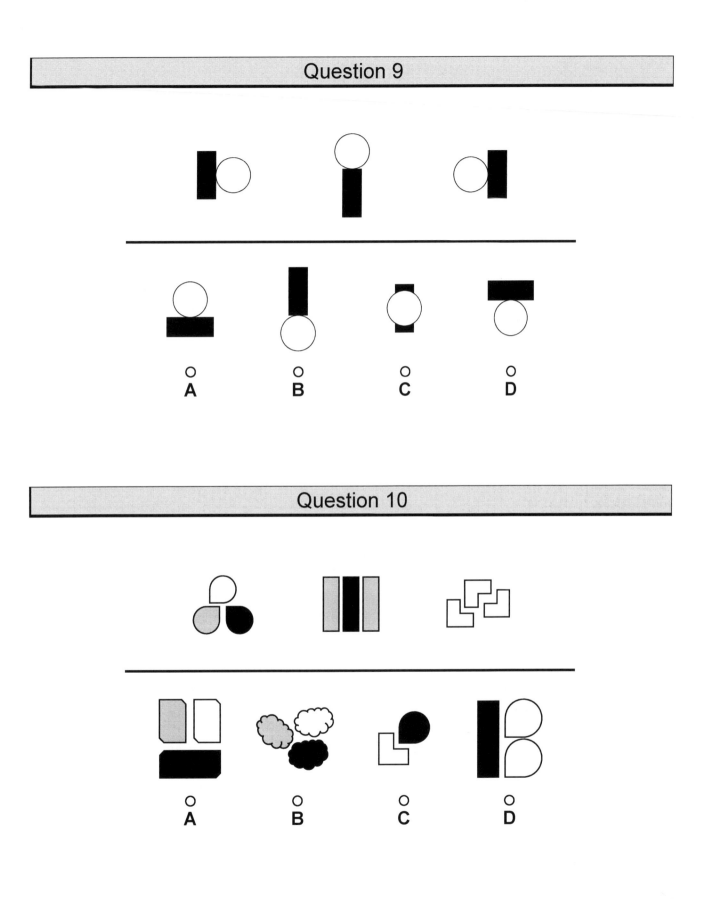

Question 10

Question 11

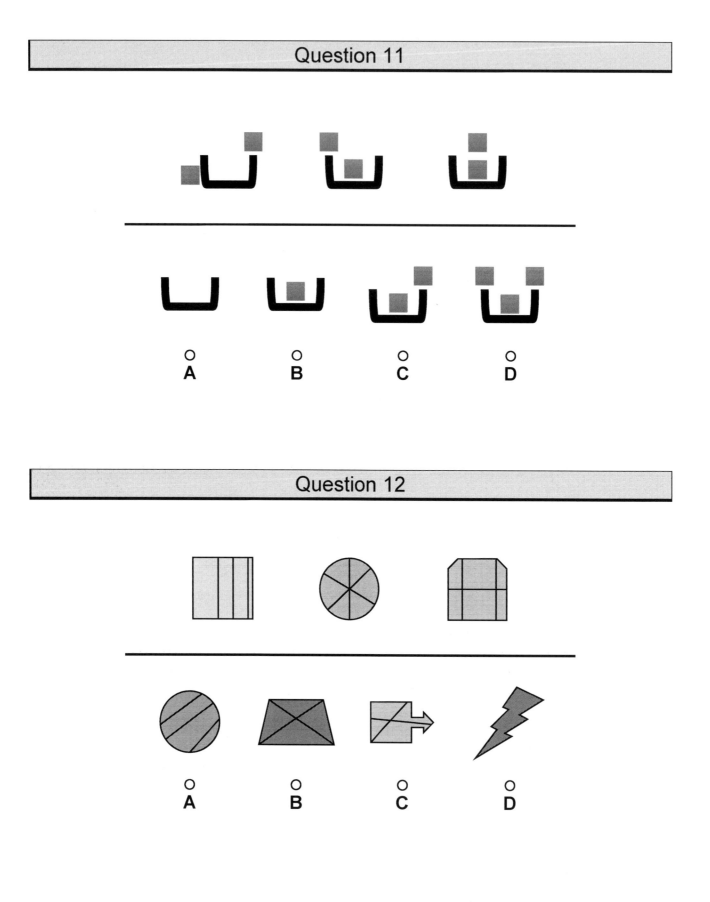

○
A

○
B

○
C

○
D

Question 12

○
A

○
B

○
C

○
D

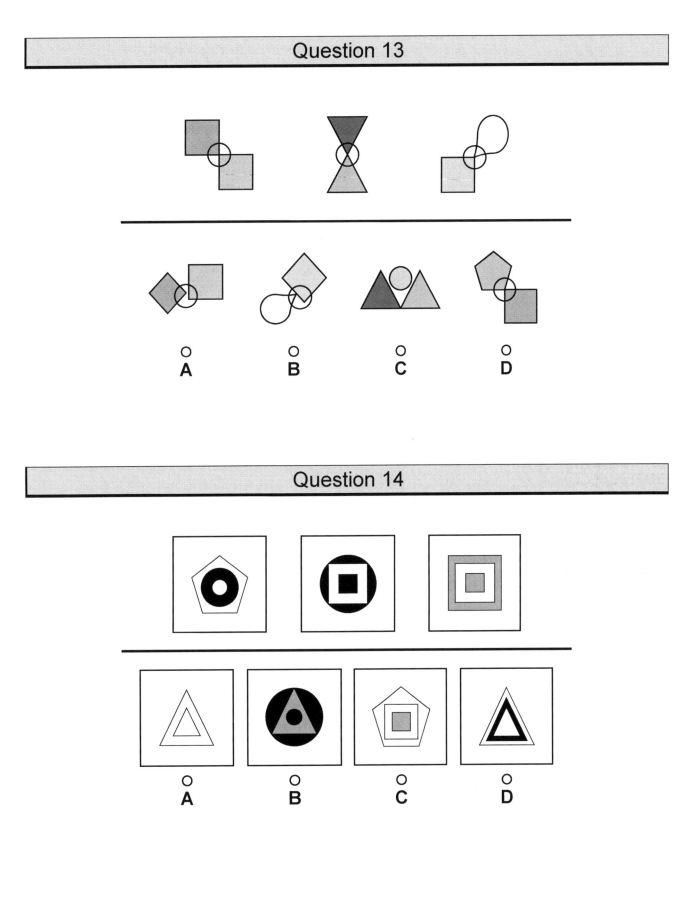

Question 13

Question 14

Question 15

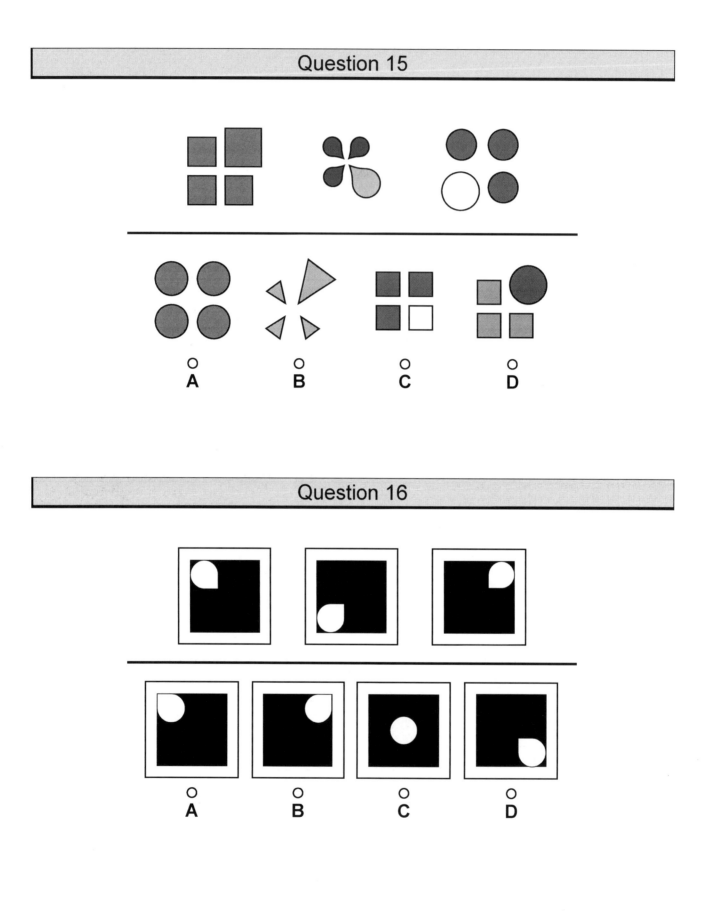

Question 16

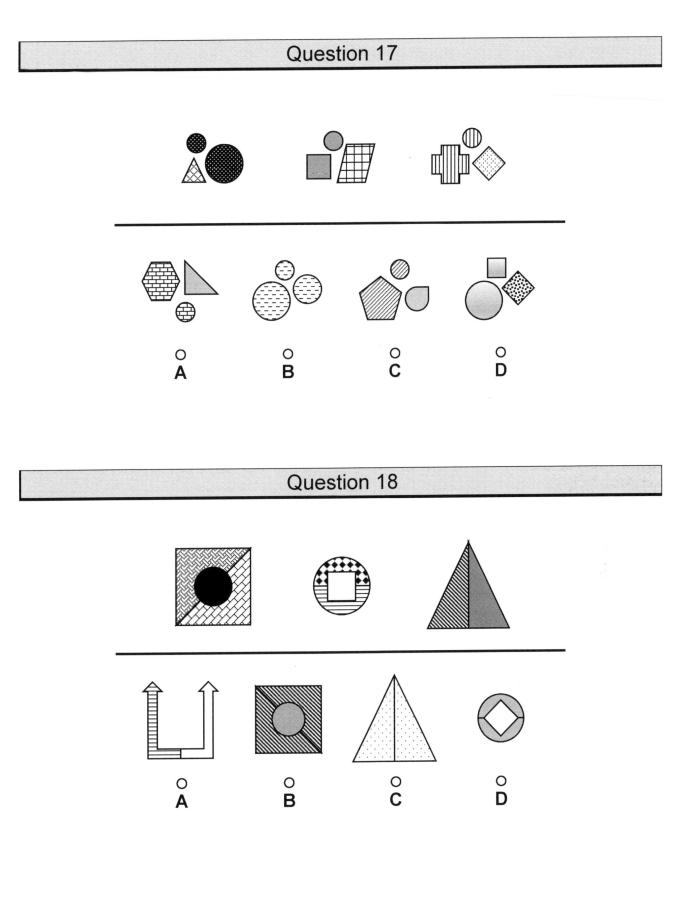

ANSWERS
& Explanations

ANSWER KEYS

Verbal Battery
Answer Key

Directions: For each question, record your answer in the column where it says "Your Answer", next to the number of the question. If your answer does not match the correct answer, mark an 'X' in the column labeled "X". Afterwards, tally the total number of incorrect answers. Subtract this amount from the total number of questions to find the total number of correct answers per subtest. Multiply the number correct by 5.56%, if there are 18 questions, or by 7.14%, if there are 14 questions, in order to get the percent correct for each subtest.

Verbal Analogies

#	Correct Answer	Your Answer	X
1	A		
2	A		
3	C		
4	B		
5	C		
6	B		
7	D		
8	D		
9	C		
10	B		
11	C		
12	A		
13	B		
14	C		
15	C		
16	D		
17	D		
18	B		

Total Incorrect: _____

Total Correct: _____

Percent Correct: _____

Sentence Completion

#	Correct Answer	Your Answer	X
1	C		
2	B		
3	B		
4	A		
5	D		
6	C		
7	D		
8	B		
9	A		
10	A		
11	C		
12	B		
13	C		
14	B		
15	A		
16	C		
17	D		
18	A		

Total Incorrect: _____

Total Correct: _____

Percent Correct: _____

Verbal Classification

#	Correct Answer	Your Answer	X
1	B		
2	B		
3	C		
4	D		
5	D		
6	D		
7	C		
8	C		
9	C		
10	B		
11	A		
12	D		
13	A		
14	A		
15	B		
16	A		
17	C		
18	D		

Total Incorrect: _____

Total Correct: _____

Percent Correct: _____

QUANTITATIVE BATTERY
Answer Key

Directions: For each question, record your answer in the column where it says "Your Answer", next to the number of the question. If your answer does not match the correct answer, mark an 'X' in the column labeled "X". Afterwards, tally the total number of incorrect answers. Subtract this amount from the total number of questions to find the total number of correct answers per subtest. Multiply the number correct by 5.56%, if there are 18 questions, or by 7.14%, if there are 14 questions, in order to get the percent correct for each subtest.

Number Analogies

#	Correct Answer	Your Answer	X
1	A		
2	C		
3	B		
4	C		
5	C		
6	D		
7	A		
8	A		
9	D		
10	B		
11	B		
12	A		
13	B		
14	C		
15	C		
16	C		
17	D		
18	A		

Number Puzzles

#	Correct Answer	Your Answer	X
1	A		
2	A		
3	A		
4	D		
5	B		
6	B		
7	C		
8	B		
9	C		
10	C		
11	A		
12	D		
13	C		
14	D		

Number Series

#	Correct Answer	Your Answer	X
1	C		
2	C		
3	B		
4	A		
5	D		
6	A		
7	B		
8	B		
9	D		
10	C		
11	D		
12	B		
13	A		
14	B		
15	D		
16	B		
17	C		
18	A		

Total Incorrect: _____   Total Incorrect: _____   Total Incorrect: _____

Total Correct: _____   Total Correct: _____   Total Correct: _____

Percent Correct: _____   Percent Correct: _____   Percent Correct: _____

NONVERBAL BATTERY
Answer Key

Directions: For each question, record your answer in the column where it says "Your Answer", next to the number of the question. If your answer does not match the correct answer, mark an 'X' in the column labeled "X". Afterwards, tally the total number of incorrect answers. Subtract this amount from the total number of questions to find the total number of correct answers per subtest. Multiply the number correct by 5.56%, if there are 18 questions, or by 7.14%, if there are 14 questions, in order to get the percent correct for each subtest.

Figure Matrices

#	Correct Answer	Your Answer	X
1	D		
2	C		
3	C		
4	A		
5	B		
6	B		
7	A		
8	C		
9	B		
10	B		
11	B		
12	A		
13	D		
14	B		
15	D		
16	C		
17	C		
18	B		

Total Incorrect: _____

Total Correct: _____

Percent Correct: _____

Paper Folding

#	Correct Answer	Your Answer	X
1	B		
2	C		
3	C		
4	C		
5	D		
6	A		
7	B		
8	C		
9	C		
10	A		
11	B		
12	D		
13	C		
14	B		

Total Incorrect: _____

Total Correct: _____

Percent Correct: _____

Figure Classification

#	Correct Answer	Your Answer	X
1	A		
2	C		
3	B		
4	D		
5	B		
6	C		
7	C		
8	B		
9	B		
10	B		
11	C		
12	A		
13	D		
14	D		
15	B		
16	D		
17	C		
18	A		

Total Incorrect: _____

Total Correct: _____

Percent Correct: _____

ANSWER
EXPLANATIONS

VERBAL BATTERY
Explanations

Verbal Analogies

1. **A**. A tadpole becomes a frog, and a caterpillar becomes a butterfly.

2. **A**. A bear lives in a cave, and a man lives in a house. C is not the correct answer because it is not specific enough, even though people do live on Earth.

3. **C**. A car drives on a road, and a train moves along tracks.

4. **B**. A candle gives off light, as does a flashlight. A pair of scissors is used for cutting, as is a knife.

5. **C**. A white circle is darkened into a black circle, so the two are color opposites. The color opposite of a black crescent moon is a white crescent moon.

6. **B**. A slice of cake is wedge-shaped. A cookie is circular. A slice of cheese is wedge-shaped, and a pie is circular.

7. **D**. A spider has 8 legs, as does an octopus. A fish has no legs, and a snake also has no legs.

8. **D**. A cow produces milk, and a bee produces honey.

9. **C**. A pen is for writing or illustrating, as is a crayon. Glue is used for pasting or putting things together, and tape is used to attach things together.

10. **B**. A cat is a mammal, and so is a bat. A dog is a mammal, and so is a cheetah.

11. **C**. The first figure shows a single sunflower, while the second figure shows a group of them. The third figure shows a balloon, so the correct answer choice is the one showing a group of balloons.

12. **A**. A witch is a symbol of Halloween, as is a ghost. Pilgrims are symbols of Thanksgiving, as is a turkey.

13. **B**. A flamingo is a type of bird, as is a penguin. The third figure shows a fish, so the correct answer should be a type of fish. Choice A is incorrect because it shows a dolphin, which is not a type of fish. Choice D is incorrect for the same reason: a whale is not a type of fish.

14. **C**. An apple is red, as are most fire trucks. A lemon is yellow, as are most school buses.

15. **C**. A basketball is intended to be shot into a basketball hoop. A golf ball is intended to be shot into a hole in a golf course.

16. **D**. The first picture shows someone languishing (feeling drained of energy) in the sun, while the second picture shows someone bundled up in winter clothes. The third picture shows an iced drink, which is more likely to be drunk when it is hot. The correct answer thus shows a drink that would be more likely to be drunk when it is cold.

17. **D**. The first picture shows a video game console controller, while the second shows someone playing video games. A controller is an essential part in playing a video game. The third picture shows a camera lens. It is an essential part of someone taking a picture. The correct answer is the silhouette of someone taking a picture. Choice A is not correct because it does not show someone using the camera or lens.

18. **B**. The first picture shows a vacuum cleaner, while the second shows a broom and dust pan. The first represents an electronic cleaning device, while the second shows equipment used in purely manual cleaning. The third picture shows a handheld fan, which is used for cooling. The correct answer shows an electronic fan. A thermostat controls the temperature, but is not itself a cooling device, so choice A is not correct. Choices C and D are not correct because they are not cooling devices. Choice C shows a mill, while choice D shows a weather vane.

Sentence Completion

1. **C**. A lamp, candle, and flashlight all provide light, but a mop does not.

2. **B**. A tractor is found on a farm. A ship, sports car, and helicopter are not ordinarily found on farms.

3. **B**. The rounder an object is, the easier it is to roll. A treasure chest is not perfectly round, so it would be the most difficult to roll.

4. **A**. Plants give off oxygen; a rock, snowflake, and bow do not give off oxygen.

5. **D**. A comb is used to straighten hair. A brush is also used to straighten hair. Choice C is not correct because a blow dryer is used to dry hair, not straighten it.

6. **C**. Not all clocks use electricity to operate. Some clocks can be wound up. All computers need electricity, as do vacuum cleaners and printers.

7. **D**. Extinct means no longer living or no longer in existence, and dinosaurs are no longer in existence.

8. **B**. Nutritious means healthy or providing nutrition. A salad is the healthiest food item among the choices. The others are considered junk food.

9. **A**. A wrench is not used for cutting; it is used for tightening or untightening objects. Scissors, saws, and knives are used mainly for cutting.

10. **A**. An entrée is a main course in a meal. A sandwich is considered the main part of a lunch. A donut is a dessert or breakfast item. Juice is a beverage, not an entrée. Cereal is a breakfast food.

11. **C**. A spatula is a cooking utensil, so it does not belong on an office desk. A comb belongs in the bathroom. A popsicle belongs in the freezer, if it's not being eaten. A stapler is used frequently in offices to attach papers or documents together, so it belongs on an office desk.

12. **B**. Flotation means floating. An anchor is not used to help float. A swimsuit does not help a person float; neither does a snorkel. A life vest does help people float.

13. **C**. An alligator or crocodile is found in a swamp, marsh, or river bank. A whale is found in the ocean or sea. A shark is also found in the ocean or sea. A frog sitting on a lily pad can be found in a pond.

14. **B**. A spoon is used for scooping up food. A pot is used for cooking. A fork is used for holding or picking up food. An egg beater is for mixing eggs.

15. **A**. Snails, crabs, and eggs all have shells. A jellyfish does not have a shell.

16. **C**. After a blizzard (which is when a lot of snow falls all at once), a shovel is needed to clear the snow. A lawnmower is used to cut the grass. A rake is usually used to clean leaves. A hose is used to provide or spray water.

17. **D**. A four-leafed clover is considered a lucky charm. A rainbow, Santa Claus, and a snowman are not considered lucky charms. A lucky charm is something you carry with you for good luck.

18. **A**. A space shuttle is the one not used directly for communication; it is used for flight and transport. Satellites, satellite dishes, and radios are all used for communication technologies.

Verbal Classification

1. **B.** The top row shows a pineapple, bananas, and grapes. These are all fruits. A strawberry is a fruit.

2. **B.** The top row shows a donkey, pig, and horse, all four-legged animals. A camel is also a four-legged animal.

3. **C.** The top row shows a bicycle, jump rope, and a football. These are all objects used to exercise. Choice C shows a dumbbell. B is not correct because it is a person swimming, which is an exercise or swimmer but not a tool used for exercise.

4. **D.** The top row shows sandals, sunglasses, and a bathing suit. These are all summer clothes items. A t-shirt is the most used during the summer.

5. **D.** The top row shows a pan, refrigerator, and blender, all tools used to work with food. Choice D shows a sieve or strainer, also used in preparing food.

6. **D.** The top row shows a stethoscope, scale, and hypodermic needle. These are all medical or health products. A Band-Aid is also a medical product.

7. **C.** The top row shows a xylophone, triangle, and drum, all percussion instruments. Choice C shows a tambourine, a percussion instrument.

8. **C.** The top row shows a teepee, castle, and igloo, all human housing types. A house is also a human home.

9. **C.** The top row shows a backpack, paper bag, and a briefcase. These are all objects used for carrying goods. Choice C is a purse, which is the closest to the items in the top row.

10. **B.** The top row shows a box, bottles, and a vault. These are all containers of some sort, used for carrying or storing goods. A shopping cart is used for carrying goods.

11. **A.** The top row shows a bed, a sleeping bag, and a crib, all things used primarily for lying down to sleep. Choice A shows a hammock, used for lying down to sleep.

12. **D.** The top row shows a sled, skis, and a skate. These are all equipment used during the winter. Choice D shows a snowboard, which is also used in the winter.

13. **A.** The top row shows a shopping cart, a wagon, and a dolly, all things used to carry items. Choice A shows a wheelbarrow, which is used to manually move items. Choices B and C are used to carry items, but they are not manually operated.

14. **A.** The top row shows a seedling (a baby plant), a tadpole (a baby frog), and a human baby. Choice A is a duckling, which is a baby duck.

15. **B.** The top row shows a stool, a car seat, and a couch. These are all things used for sitting on. Choice B shows an ottoman, which is also used for sitting.

16. **A.** The top row shows items associated with birthday parties. A gift is also associated with birthdays.

17. **C.** The top row shows a clapperboard, video camera, and film. All of these things are essential, or were at one point essential, to the production of movies and shows. Thus, the correct answer also has to be something essential to the production of movies. Choice C shows stage lights, which are essential to the production of movies. Choice A shows a director's seat, but it is not considered a vital part of movie production, since a director could still conduct a movie while standing up.

18. **D.** The top row shows a football helmet, safety goggles, and a catcher's mitt. These are all forms of protective gear. Choice D shows knee pads, which are a type of protective gear. A baseball bat, whistle, and hockey puck are equipment used in sports, but they are not for protection. A whistle, in some cases, is used for protection, but whistles are not worn in the same fashion that the other items would be worn. Choice D is still the stronger answer.

QUANTITATIVE BATTERY
Explanations

Number Analogies

1. **A.** A pizza is reduced to half of a pizza, so an orange should be reduced to half of an orange.

2. **C.** 1 fish increases to 2 fish (1 + 1 = 2), so 2 turtles should increase to 3 (2 + 1 = 3) turtles.

3. **B.** 3 circles are decreased to 1 (3 – 2 = 1), so 4 squares should be decreased to 2 (4 – 2 = 2).

4. **C.** Half an egg is increased to one whole egg, so half a sandwich should be increased to a whole sandwich.

5. **C.** There are 2 strawberries in the first figure and 2 cherries in the second. The number remains the same, while the type of object changes. The third figure is of 3 daisies, so the correct answer should have 3 objects of a different type.

6. **D.** 1 elephant is increased to 2 (1 + 1 = 2), so 3 ladybugs should be increased to 4 (3 + 1 = 4).

7. **A.** 16 clovers are reduced to 4. Since there aren't more than 12 suns to reduce, look for another relationship. We can also see that there are 4 sets of 4 clovers in the first figure. The correct answer is 1 sun because 4 sets of 1 sun gives 4 suns.

8. **A.** 2 plums are doubled to 4 plums, so 1 banana is doubled to 2. You can't make an addition problem out of this; 1 + 2 = 3, but 3 bananas is not an answer choice.

9. **D.** The number of leaves equals the number of dots on the die. The correct answer is 2 snails because the number of dots on the die in the third figure is 2.

10. **B.** 1 lemon is increasing to 1 and a half lemons. Take half a lemon and add it to 1 to get 1 and a half. Half of 2 books is 1 book, so when you add 1 book to 2 books, you get 3 books.

11. **B.** 2 pencils are reduced in half to 1 pencil. When 4 crayons are reduced in half, you get 2 crayons.

12. **A.** The first house has 2 windows, while the second house has 1 window. The number of windows decreases by 1. A tricycle has 3 wheels. If you take away 1 wheel, you get a bicycle, which has 2 wheels.

13. **B.** 3 stars are increased to 5 (3 + 2 = 5), so 1 heart is increased to 3 (1 + 2 = 3).

14. **C.** 1 shirt is increased to 3, so 2 socks are increased to 6 (3 pairs of socks is 6 socks).

15. **C.** 5 segments are reduced to 1, so 5 pears are reduced to 1 pear.

16. **C.** 1 lightning bolt is increased to 4, so 1 segment is increased to 4.

17. **D.** The first square shows 9 teddy bears. The second shows a square, which has 4 sides. The difference between 9 and 4 is 5. The third figure shows a heptagon, which has 7 sides. The correct answer will have either 2 teddy bears or 12 because 7 – 5 = 2, and 12 – 7 = 5. None of the answer choices contains 2 teddy bears, so the only possible choice is D, which has 12.

18. **A.** The first square shows 5 circles, and the second square shows 3 triangles, so there is a difference of 2 objects. The third square shows 3 squares, so the correct answer will have either 1 (3 – 2 = 1) object or 5 (3 + 2 = 5). Since choice A shows 1 object and choice C shows 5 objects, both might work. The better answer, however, is A. To get from the number in the first square (5) to the number in the second square (3), we had to subtract 2 (5 – 2 = 3) objects. Thus, it is more analogically correct to subtract 2 from the number of objects in the third square. In other words, 3 – 2 = 1. Don't be fooled by the way the question is set up; the question is not 4 objects to 3 objects, and we know this because none of the answer choices contains 2 (3 – 1) or 4 (3 + 1) objects.

Number Puzzles

1. **A.** The first train has 5 dots. The second train has 4, so it needs 1 more to make 5 (4 + 1 = 5).

2. **A.** The first train has 7 dots. The second train has 2, so it needs 5 more to make 7 (2 + 5 = 7).

3. **A.** The first train has 5 dots. The second train has 3, so it needs 2 more to make 5 (3 + 2 = 5).

4. **D.** The first train has 4 dots. The second train has 4, so it needs 0 more to make 4 (4 + 0 = 4).

5. **B.** The first train has 6 dots. The second train has 4, so it needs 2 more to make 6 (4 + 2 = 6).

6. **B.** The first train has 4 dots. The second train has 2, so it needs 2 more to make 4 (2 + 2 = 4).

7. **C.** The first train has 8 dots. The second train has 1, so it needs 7 more to make 8 (1 + 7 = 8).

8. **B.** The first train has 7 dots. The second train has 2, so it needs 5 more to make 7 (2 + 5 = 7).

9. **C.** The first train has 7 dots. The second train has 3, so it needs 4 more to make 7 (3 + 4 = 7).

10. **C.** The first train has 8 dots. The second train has 3, so it needs 5 more to make 8 (3 + 5 = 8).

11. **A.** The first train has 10 dots. The second train has 5, so it needs 5 more to make 10 (5 + 5 = 10).

12. **D.** The first train has 6 dots. The second train has 3, so it needs 3 more to make 6 (3 + 3 = 6).

13. **C.** The first train has 11 dots. The second train has 5, so it needs 6 more to make 11 (5 + 6 = 11).

14. **D.** The first train has 9 dots. The second train has 4, so it needs 5 more to make 11 (4 + 5 = 9).

Number Series

1. **C.** The pattern is 5, 5, 5, 5, 5, 6. There are 5 columns with 5 beads. The 6th column has 6 beads, so the next column will also have 6 beads.

2. **C.** The pattern is 2, 2, 3, 3, 4, 4. Each number repeats twice, and then goes up by 1, so the next number is 5.

3. **B.** The pattern is 5, 6, 7, 8, 8, 7. After going up in number to 8, 8 repeats once and then starts going back down. The next column after 7 should be 6.

4. **A.** The pattern is 5, 3, 5, 3, 5, 3. The pattern alternates between 5 and 3, so the number after 3 should be 5.

5. **D.** The pattern is 4, 2, 1, 4, 2, 1. The pattern repeats after 3 numbers, so the next number should be 4.

6. **A.** The pattern is 8, 6, 4, 2, 3, 5. At first the pattern decreases by 2. After getting to 2, it increases. The first increase is by 1, and the second increase is by 2, so the next increase is by 3 to get 5 + 3 = 8.

7. **B.** The pattern is 2, 1, 2, 3, 2, 1. After the number decreases to 1, it starts goes up again until it reaches 3. After reaching 3, it goes down to 1. The next number should be 2 (1 + 1 = 2).

8. **B.** The pattern is 3, 4, 4, 4, 3, 4. The pattern is three 4s after a 3, so the next number should be 4.

9. **D.** The pattern is 1, 3, 3, 4, 5, 5. There are 2 patterns here. The first is: 1, 3, 5 (+ 2; odd columns). The second pattern is: 3, 4, 5 (− 1; even columns). The next number is in an odd column, so 5 + 2 = 7.

10. **C.** The pattern is 2, 1 ,2, 4, 8, 4. The pattern halves when it is decreasing and doubles when it is increasing. Since the pattern is decreasing, the next number is half of 4, which is 2.

11. **D.** The pattern is 2, 4, 4, 3, 6, 2. There are 2 patterns. The first is: 2, 4, 6 (+ 2; odd columns). The second pattern is: 4, 3, 1 (− 1; even columns). The next number is in an odd column, 6 + 2 = 8.

12. **B.** The pattern is 4, 5, 5, 4, 6, 3. There are 2 patterns. The first is: 4, 5, 6 (+ 1; odd columns). The second is: 5, 4, 3 (− 1; even columns). The next is in an odd column; 6 + 1 = 7.

13. **A.** The pattern is 1, 2, 2, 3, 3, 3. The pattern is that there are the same number of columns as the number of beads. Since there were already 3 columns of 3 beads, the next has 4.

14. **B.** The pattern is 1, 3, 2, 3, 1, 3. There are 2 patterns. The first is: 1, 2, 1, going between 1 and 2 (odd columns). The second pattern is: 3, 3, 3 (even columns). The next number is in an odd column, so it should be 2.

15. **D.** The pattern is 4, 2, 0, 4, 2, 0. The pattern repeats after 3 numbers, so the next number should be 4, to start the pattern again.

16. **B.** The pattern is 3, 2, 4, 3, 5, 4. There are 2 patterns. The first is: 3, 4, 5 (+ 1; odd columns). The second is: 2, 3, 4 (+ 1; even columns). The next is in an odd column; 5 + 1 = 6.

17. **C.** The pattern is 0, 1, 1, 2, 3, 5. Except for the first two columns, all of the other columns contain the same number of beads as the number of beads in the previous two columns put together. The next column will therefore contain 8 beads, since 5 + 3 = 8.

18. **A.** Every column contains 6 beads. It's a matter of how the beads are arranged. The first four columns show the bottom set of beads increasing by 1 with each column move to the right and the top set of beads decreasing by 1. The fifth column shows a 3,3 split again, but the sixth column shows the opposite pattern of the second column, in that now the number of beads is decreasing when moving to the right. Thus, the next column should show a 5, 1 split, with the 1 bead on the bottom and 5 on top.

NONVERBAL BATTERY

Explanations

Figure Matrices

1. **D**. The first two figures have 5 sides each. The third figure has 6 sides, so the correct answer is D.

2. **C**. The second figure is a smaller version of the first figure. Choice C is the best answer because the size matches that of the second figure.

3. **C**. The second figure is a larger version of the first figure. The correct answer is C, a larger version of the circle in the third figure.

4. **A**. The second figure is the first figure but narrower. Choice A is a narrower version of the third figure.

5. **B**. The second figure is the first figure that has been rotated 90° counterclockwise. Choice B is the third figure is rotated 90° counterclockwise.

6. **B**. The second figure shows a box around the first figure with the colors inverted. Choice B is a box around the third figure with the colors inverted.

7. **A**. The second figure is double the first figure, and the ends are joined. Choice A is double the first figure and the ends are joined together.

8. **C**. The second figure is a three-dimensional version of the first figure. The answer choice is a three-dimensional version of the third figure.

9. **B**. The second figure is the first figure that has been rotated clockwise 45°. Choice B is the third figure rotated clockwise 45°.

10. **B**. The second figure has 5 sides, while the first figure has 6 sides. The third figure has 8 sides, so the answer choice should have 7 sides.

11. **B**. The second figure is half of the first figure. Choice B is half of the third figure. Choice C is not correct because the shading is incorrect.

12. **A**. The second figure is a mirror reflection of the first. Choice A is a mirror reflection of the third figure.

13. **D**. The second figure has a smaller version of the first figure partially overlaid on top of the first figure. Choice D shows a smaller version of the third figure overlaid partially on top of the third figure.

14. **B**. The second figure shows the left shape (triangle) of the first figure placed on top of the right shape (square) of the first figure. Choice B shows the left shape (square) of the third figure placed on top of the right shape (circle) of the third figure.

15. **D**. The second figure shows the first figure with the shading inverted and darkened. Choice D shows the third figure inverted with darker shading.

16. **C**. The second figure shows the first two shapes (circle and trapezoid) of the first figure switching positions. When the first two shapes (triangle and triangle) of the third figure switch positions, you get Choice C.

17. **C**. The second figure shows the first figure reduced in size and rotated 45° clockwise. Choice C shows the third figure reduced in size and rotated clockwise 45°. Tip: Rotate the paper and notice the lines of the square. Because the square in the third figure is shaded by lines running parallel to the top and bottom sides of the square, those lines should always stay parallel to the top and bottom sides of the square.

18. **B**. The second figure shows a smaller first figure with another object added to the right side of it. Specifically, the first figure is a pentagon, which has 5 sides. A square larger than the smaller pentagon, which has 4 sides, or 1 fewer side than the pentagon, is attached to the pentagon in the second figure. The third figure shows a square. Choice B shows a smaller version of the square (4 sides) attached to a triangle (3 sides, or 1 fewer side than a square) larger than the reduced square.

Paper Folding

1. **B**. The paper is folded once, so there will be a total of 2 holes, as shown:

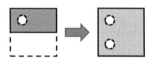

2. **C**. The paper is folded once, so there will be a total of 6 holes, as shown:

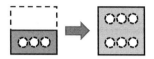

3. **C**. The paper is folded once, so there will be a total of 4 holes, as shown:

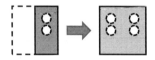

4. **C**. The paper is folded once, so there will be a total of 4 holes.

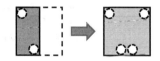

5. **D**. The paper is folded twice, so there will be a total of 4 holes, as shown:

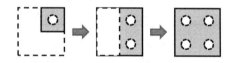

6. **A**. The paper is folded twice, so there will be a total of 8 holes, as shown:

7. **B**. The paper is folded twice, so there will be a total of 8 holes, as shown:

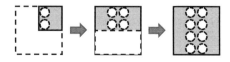

8. **C**. The paper is folded twice, so there will be a total of 4 holes, as shown:

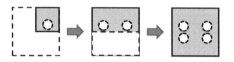

9. **C**. The paper is folded once, so there will be a total of 6 holes, as shown:

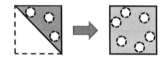

10. **A**. The paper is folded twice, so there will be a total of 4 holes, as shown:

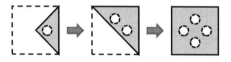

11. **B**. The paper is folded twice, so there will be a total of 4 holes, as shown:

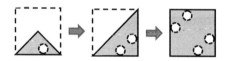

12. **D**. The paper is folded once, so there will be a total of 6 holes, as shown:

13. **C**. The paper is folded three times, so there will be a total of 8 holes, as shown:

14. **B**. The paper is folded three times, so there will be a total of 8 holes, as shown:

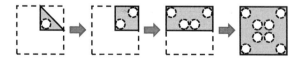

Figure Classification

1. **A**. The figures in the top row all have 4 sides. Choice A has 4 sides.

2. **C**. The figures in the top row each has a straight line drawn vertically (up and down) in the middle. Choice C has a vertical line drawn down the middle.

3. **B**. The figures in the top row all have two shapes that are vertical mirror reflections of each other. Choice B shows two shapes that are mirror reflections of each other.

4. **D**. The figures in the top row all have a smaller shaded square in a corner of a larger square. Choice D fits this description.

5. **B**. The figures in the top row all have some roundness. Choice B shows some roundness.

6. **C**. The figures in the top row all have two circles and a straight line intersecting or touching the two circles. Choice C shows two circles that have a straight line passing through them.

7. **C**. The figures in the top row all have a smaller white shape nested into a larger, similar shaded shape. Choice C shows a smaller heart nested into a larger heart. The larger heart is shaded and the smaller heart is white.

8. **B**. The figures in the top row all have two lines that intersect. Choice B shows two lines that intersect.

9. **B**. The figures in the top row show a vertical black bar and a white circle next to attached to a side of the bar. Choice B shows a vertical black bar with a white circle attached to one of the sides of the black bar.

10. **B**. The figures in the top row show three shapes of equal size. Choice B shows three clouds of equal size.

11. **C**. The figures in the top row show the outline of a container with two squares in or next to it.

Choice C shows the outline of a container with two squares in or next to it.

12. **A**. The figures in the top row show figures with three lines drawn through the figures. Choice A shows a circle with three lines drawn through it.

13. **D**. The figures in the top row show two shapes touching at a vertex (corner) with a circle around the point of contact. Choice D shows a pentagon and a square meeting with a circle around the point of contact.

14. **D**. The figures in the top row have three shapes, but the inside two shapes are the same, except that the innermost shape is the same shade as the outermost shape. Choice D is the one that meets the requirements.

15. **B**. The figures in the top row have four of the same shape, except that one of the shapes is larger. Choice B shows four triangles, with one bigger than the rest.

16. **D**. The figures show a black square with a teardrop shape in the corner, with the round part facing the corner. Choice D meets these requirements.

17. **C**. The figures in the top row all have a small circle on top. For each figure, the circle is shaded in the same way as one other shape is. There are at least 2 different shapes and shading styles for each figure. Choice C is the only one that meets all of these requirements. Choice A is incorrect because the circle is at the bottom. Choice B is incorrect because all three shapes are circles and there is only one shading style. Choice D is incorrect because it doesn't have a small circle at the top.

18. **A**. Each figure in the top row shows a figure being divided into two regions. Each region of each figure is shaded differently than the others are. Choice A is the only figure that meets these requirements.

Made in the USA
Monee, IL
30 September 2021